Daniel Harrison Jacques

The temperaments;

Or, The varieties of physical constitution in man, considered in their relations to

mental character and the practical affairs of life, etc., etc.

Daniel Harrison Jacques

The temperaments;
Or, The varieties of physical constitution in man, considered in their relations to mental character and the practical affairs of life, etc., etc.

ISBN/EAN: 9783337717483

Printed in Europe, USA, Canada, Australia, Japan

Cover: Foto ©ninafisch / pixelio.de

More available books at **www.hansebooks.com**

THE

TEMPERAMENTS;

OR,

THE VARIETIES OF

PHYSICAL CONSTITUTION IN MAN,

CONSIDERED IN THEIR RELATIONS

TO

MENTAL CHARACTER

AND THE

PRACTICAL AFFAIRS OF LIFE, ETC., ETC.

BY D. H. JACQUES, M.D.

WITH AN INTRODUCTION

BY H. S. DRAYTON. A M

THE

TEMPERAMENTS;

OR,

THE VARIETIES OF

PHYSICAL CONSTITUTION IN MAN,

CONSIDERED IN THEIR RELATIONS

TO

MENTAL CHARACTER

AND THE

PRACTICAL AFFAIRS OF LIFE, ETC., ETC.

BY D. H. JACQUES, M.D.

WITH AN INTRODUCTION

BY H. S. DRAYTON, A.M.,
EDITOR OF THE "PHRENOLOGICAL JOURNAL, ETC."

NEW YORK:
FOWLER & WELLS CO., PUBLISHERS,
775 BROADWAY.
1888.

CONTENTS.

(iii)

V.

VI.

VII.

VIII.

IX.

X.

XI.

INTRODUCTION.

THE literature of the Temperaments is very scanty If the physiologist or student of human nature will survey the field from the time even of Hippocrates, he will be astonished by the paucity of authors who have given to the world aught in the way of observations or speculations on the nature and characteristic influence of the physical constitution expressed by the term Temperament. Indeed, he may count the treatises known to the world upon his fingers. This singular fact can not be imputed to a lack of information on the subject, for the medicists of the times of Hippocrates and Galen held certain well-defined views concerning peculiar conditions or diatheses of the human body, and the vocation of the physician necessarily required him to consider in some way the mental and physical constitution of his patients, and to adapt his treatment, whatever it might be, to their systemic habits. What is found in the old Greek and Latin authors savors much, to be sure, of dogma, but there is so much of definiteness in their characterization, as in the case of the quartic classification of Hippocrates, that we are led to believe that their knowledge of human physiology, or of the principles governing growth and organic function, was really more positive and nearer practical exactness

than appears in most of their discussions of disease and its treatment. Speculation, however, characterized the medical thought of the ancient and
medieval periods, just as it predominated in the discussions concerning the nature of the mind and the
relation of the thinking principle to the brain or the
physical organism. If one will follow the lines of
thought as crystallized in the works on medicine and
metaphysics which have survived the lapse of ages,
he will observe that a parallelism exists between these
two great branches of inquiry, and that progress or
development in one, is accompanied by advancement
in the other. The great period of illumination in
physiology which was ushered in by Harvey's dem-
onstration of the movement of the blood, had its
complement in the long stride made by modern research in nervous function and the office of the brain
—of which research the Oxford professor, Willis, was
one of the chief promoters.

When science had fairly emerged from the maze
of medieval controversy, and chemistry, astronomy,
physiology, and mental philosophy had been established upon firm principles universally recognized,
then the wonderful development of the eighteenth
and nineteenth centuries was begun. In this development we perceive the influence of Temperament,
and it is no difficult task for the physiologist, particularly if he be learned in the works of Gall and Spurzheim, to signalize the several effects which peculiar
constitutional states have had in determining the
course of individual effort and in molding results.

It would, therefore, appear that the subject of this
treatise is an important one ; in fact, one of the most

important within the province of the student and author; but to indicate in this place, in more than a few points, the nature of that importance, would be to trespass upon the field which Dr. Jacques has covered with that fullness of detail which evidences his familiarity with the subject as a student and trained observer, and in that graceful, instructive style which has made his well-known treatises on popular education and physiology so acceptable wherever they have been read.

Every living organism has certain qualities by which it is distinguished as belonging to a certain class, order, or species of organisms. The naturalist has taken upon himself the labor of analyzing and defining the myriad forms of being, and for centuries has found a most fruitful field for the exercise of his intellectual powers. He finds his task one of infinite extensibility; with each attainment of knowledge new vistas of research open before him; and in lines where he had believed there was little remaining for scrutiny, he is often amazed by the opening up of a fresh mine, which invites his enthusiastic investigation. He has found the domain of life so vast that he must needs devote himself to but a few members of the animal or vegetable world, would he learn m ch of their peculiarities in the short space allotted him for active labor on earth. He perceives that his work is complicated, not only by the apparent crossings and mixtures of species, but also by variations in the constitution peculiar to members of species. To him the worm and the beetle have their family characteristics of color and form, as well as the lion, horse, or dog; and he pries into their homes and

habits to ascertain the sources and reasons for such
characteristics.

The physiologist who has chosen man for his study
finds the subject to unfold rapidly before his con-
templation, until it becomes a maze of complication ;
its web of moral, intellectual, and physical interrela-
tion assuming a thousand hues and forms as he views
it.   In despair of ever tracing every line to its source
and revealing the secret springs of human mental
and moral life, he may well exclaim with the great
dramatist, " What a piece of work is man !   How
noble in reason ! how infinite in faculties ! "

The primary influence or property in living organisms, is that known by the term Heredity.   Its essence
is unattainable by the nicest methods of the chemist,
inexplicable by the most careful analysis of the philosopher.   Creative energy supplies it ; creative wis-
dom only can resolve it.   Let the physiologist con-
cern himself with the effects of this hereditary,
this differential vital force, in their manifold forms.
He has, to be sure, already acquired a large store of
facts in such study; let him go on with his observation and research.   Turning aside, now and then, to
look into the marvelous evolutions of the protoplas-
mic germ with the hope of attaining the why and
wherefore, while the organized forms are not yet
fully comprehended in their commonest phases of
activity, is but wasting time and talent, and neg-
lecting the useful.

In the study of the human Temperaments the
physiologist who elects it is brought to the consideration of the effects of inheritance, and, subse-
quently, in addition, of habit upon the body and

the mind. He early perceives the vast importance of a correct understanding of the physical organization, the functional peculiarities of stomach, heart, and lungs; the quality of brain; the contour and texture of bone, muscle, and tissue in individual cases. Man is many-sided, exceedingly versatile in his range of capability, and his highest, truest success is found in relations where his body and mind are harmoniously employed; where, in other words, he finds a complete adaptation of his powers, mental and physical.

So far as concerns themselves, every man and woman should be physiologists, should be conversant with the laws and processes of their physical nature; not merely knowing something of the mode by which food enters the stomach and is converted into nutriment, or how the blood passes from the heart to the lungs and is vitalized by respiration, but how they differ from other men and women in constitution of body and properties of mind, and what the differences mean in relation to individual capability. The great majority of intelligent workers in every sphere of life are misplaced, and, therefore, fail to accomplish as much for themselves and the world as they would in their appropriate departments of effort. This fact is appreciated by thousands who discovered too late their unfitness for the vocation which a parent, or caprice, or necessity assigned to them; while other thousands are toiling sadly and wearily amid inharmonious relations, attributing their unsuccess to ill-luck or destiny, and totally unaware of the fundamental cause of their unfortunate situation.

Whether the physiologist makes his analysis in accordance with the old system of four Temperaments, or in accordance with the new system, which recognizes but three, he attributes a certain type of organization to the person under his observation. He does not expect the man in whom the nervous or mental quality predominates, to exhibit the disposition of the man in whom the bilious or motive quality is the most conspicuous. And he would not assign men so differently constituted to the same kind of work, any more than an experienced agriculturist would set a plow and cultivator side by side in a rough field, and expect them to perform similar duty in preparing the soil for a crop. No; he would assign to him of the strong mental or nervous constitution work which required the exercise chiefly of the intellect and a light, facile hand; while to him of the motive or bilious type, he would give labor requiring muscular strength and steady, enduring application; for one he would consider the duties of the counting-room or office appropriate; for the other the tasks of the farm or the workshop.

He would not think of supplying these two men with food of like materials and quantity, because he knows that their differences in physical constitution enjoin a difference in their food, which must be observed for the maintenance of their respective healths. And further still, their proclivities and requirements are unlike, as he perceives, in the matter of recreation, society, and mental avocation.

This subject of Temperament, the reader may remark, is one which relates mainly to the human body, how it is built up and constituted in its different parts;

it particularly relates to the office or influence exer
cised in the economy of physical life by those great
organs—the stomach, liver, lungs, heart, brain, and
nerves. Yes, this is true if we merely consider the
bodily constitution as a piece of vitalized mechanism :
but the study of the human Temperaments is vastly
more than a department of mechanical physiology, and
relates, as we have indicated, to the part man fills as the
most powerful factor in the economy of nature. We
can not assert that man is what he is by virtue of his
physical organization, yet the potency of Temperament may not be estimated, and we can not separate
man's psychic susceptibilities and capabilities, in their
practical analysis, from his physical constitution. The
latter supplements the former—body feeds mind. The
subtile connection between mind and body can not
be explained any more than that agent or force which
we so glibly call life ; to comprehend one would be
to comprehend the other ; yet when we examine the
material aspects of the human machine, the body,
we are guided to safe conclusions with respect to the
operation of that machine ; we are enabled to judge
of its productive energy in both physical and mental
respects. If the appreciation of phenomena be the
proper domain of science, it seems to us clear enough
that, when taken on its material side only, there can
be a no more interesting subject for the research of
the earnest scientific inquirer than this of the Temperaments. Comparatively fresh as a department of
study, it possesses every feature of attraction, every
quality of interest, appealing to the imagination as
well as to the judgment, and furnishing an exhaust-
less stock of materials. The student, moreover, needs

not to travel to the East or to the West, for at his
very door, in his home-circle, and among the friends
who surround him, is a world upon which he may ex-
pend the resources of his intellect, and to his profit
and theirs.   It is said that an eminent German naturalist occupied the greater part of thirty years in
studying the nature of a single species of worm, and
declared that he had by no means learned all there is
to be ascertained about it.   What, then, is to be said
of the study of human nature, the highest form of
life, with its myriad phases of contour and its com-
plex mental and physical correlations!

The earnest observer in this field may well pause
in amazement as some reflection concerning its vast-
ness is suggested to his mind; but aided by the results of the labor of others, guided by those principles which genius has deduced, he can pursue his way
through the apparent confusion and grasp fact after
fact, and add truth after truth to his store of useful
knowledge.

With a cordial appreciation of the need of a popular treatise on the Temperaments, this volume has
been carefully prepared.   The extent of the subject
precludes anything like an exhaustive attempt, yet
the author has striven to consider it from all practical sides, and to arrange his data in such a manner
that the student may find it of service as a guide in
personal observations.   The illustrations, with but
a very few exceptions, are from life—in fact, carefully
engraved portraits—so that their value in a scientific
respect is positive.   It is unnecessary to state, perhaps, that the introduction of every portrait is simply
for the purpose of illustrating the text, and, there-

fore, the only motive in their use is a purely scientific one. As the originals of some of the portraits are living, this statement is deemed expedient as an explanation or apology for their appearance.

Shortly after completing this work Dr. Jacques laid down his pen forever. Death came suddenly while he was at his residence in Fernandina, Florida. Well-advanced in life, yet not old; in the midst of his usefulness—a usefulness founded upon a life of great variety and activity, in whose scenes he carried a studious mind and an unusual calmness of judgment, which enabled him to profit by every experience, it is not strange that his death awakened deep regret in the wide circle for which he had become a highly respected adviser. Few men of his age have contributed as much as he to practical educational literature. · He studied and observed for the purpose of obtaining information which he could disseminate broadly through the press. He was a writer by profession, and filled, in the course of forty years or more, many responsible positions, as editor, author, and contributor. For many years his pen was of valuable service to the *Phrenological Journal,* and other well-known magazines were indebted to him for important contributions to their pages. He loved the country, and was at home in the field and garden, and during the past ten years his literary services were chiefly given to agriculture. The *Rural Carolinian* the *Semi-Tropical,* and the other leading agricultural magazines of the South, found in him their strongest ally. His opinions were authoritative, although he never sought to exercise authority in any sphere. He loved the quiet reserve of home; his spirit had no

1*

sympathy for the rude and turbulent ; he was content
to stand apart from the busy current of the world's
business, and simply contemplate its ever-changing
surface. But it was as a keen observer that he
looked upon the swaying masses of humanity; his
massive perceptive faculties descried new and valuable things where the ordinary spectator saw nothing
but commonplace events ; and so he went on from
year to year accumulating data, and in the retirement
of his library recording them with a facile pen for the
instruction of the people. His " Manuals for Home
Improvement," " The Right Word in the Right
Place," and " Physical Perfection," are models of
literary style and of didactic method, and are not
surpassed by any books in print in just adaptation
to the wants of the masses. Although produced
years ago, they are fresh to-day as practical personal educators, and their worth enhances in the
proportion of their circulation.

Dr. Jacques was not of those who " make a noise
in the world," he did not covet notice, and beyond a
narrow circle of sympathetic friends and *littérateurs*
he was scarcely known personally, but his work will
remain long after the noisy thousands have been forgotten, its solid benefits making society his debtor.

H. S. DRAYTON,

Editor of the Phrenological Journal.

THE TEMPERAMENTS.

I.

THE HUMAN BODY AND ITS FUNCTIONS.

As Temperament, considered in its physical aspects, s a state of the body depending upon certain combinations of its various systems of organs and certain functional conditions affecting them, some knowledge or these organs and their functions will be essential to the profitable study of the subject before us. For this knowledge in its details, we must refer the reader, not already familiar with them, to the standard works on Anatomy and Physiology; but, in order that he may have at hand, for easy reference, the general facts pertaining to the human physical organization, we shall here devote a few pages to the presentation of such outlines as will, we trust, serve the purpose in view. We condense from previous works, claiming no originality for the general features of our sketch.

We find in the human body three grand classes or systems of organs, each of which has its special function in the general economy. They may appropriately be called—

 1. The Motive or Mechanical System;
 2. The Vital or Nutritive System; and
 3. The Mental or Nervous System.

These three systems, each naturally divided into several branches, include all the organs and perform all the functions of the physical man.

I.—THE MOTIVE OR MECHANICAL SYSTEM.

The motive or mechanical system consists of three sets of organs, forming, in combination, an apparatus of *levers* through which locomotion and all the larger movements of the body are effected. They are:

1. The Bones;
2. The Ligaments; and
3. The Muscles.

1. *The Bones.*—The Bones form the framework of the body. They are primarily organs of support, sustaining and giving solidity to every part. The proportion which they bear to their fleshy covering differs materially in different individuals; and this fact should be remembered as having an important bearing upon the doctrine of the Temperaments, to be unfolded in future chapters.

In the earlier stages of their formation, the bones are cartilaginous or gristly in their structures, very flexible, and not easily broken. This wise provision of an all-wise Nature is illustrated in young children, whose innumerable falls never result in a fracture, and whose rapid growth would be entirely inconsistent with a hardened osseous frame. We may note here, too, in passing, that the legs of infants are often made permanently crooked by being required, under the injudicious training of unwisely ambitious parents, to support prematurely the weight of the body. Little is gained by interfering with Nature, in such attempts to hasten her processes.

In due time the bones, receiving deposits of lime, phosphorus, and other earthy materials, gradually harden, and at their maturity are composed of nearly equal proportions of animal and mineral matter. In old age the earthy matter often greatly predominates, rendering them very brittle.

Like other parts of the body, the bones have a system of blood-vessels and nerves, and, like the other parts, are subject to growth and decay, though their changes are less rapid than those of the softer parts. Their minute structure is very curious and beautiful.

The genius and skill of man has never yet succeeded in constructing a machine so beautiful in its perfect adaptation to its uses as the human skeleton; nor can the wisest of mortals suggest an improvement in its structure.

See what noble twin columns, resting upon the firm, but flexible bases of the feet, support, in its proper position, the grand arch of the pelvis! And the pelvis itself, how admirably adapted to its various functions! While it has all the necessary strength to support the body which rests upon it, it is not less perfectly adapted to protect and sustain the vital organs situated within it, and to afford them room for the proper performance of their functions.

The grand central pillar, the spinal column, on whose capital rests that sublime "dome of thought," the cranium, has its base on the sacrum, a wedge-like bone which forms the keystone of the pelvic arch. The spinal or vertebral column itself is one of the most wonderful of Nature's wonderful works. It is composed of twenty-four bones, called vertebræ, linked firmly together by a complicated system of ligaments, giving it immense strength, and, at the same time, great flexibility. It is pierced by what is called the vertebral canal, through which passes the spinal cord (*medulla spinalis*), of which we shall have more to say further on.

Attached to the dorsal or back vertebræ by strong ligaments, and bending forward so as to form the grand cavity of the thorax, are the twenty-four ribs, twelve on each side. The uppermost seven on each side are called the true ribs, because each of them is connected by a separate cartilage directly with the sternum or breast bone ; while the lower five are called false, because one or two of them are loose at the anterior extremity and the cartilages of the rest run into each other, instead of being separately prolonged to the breast bone.

The arms are loosely attached to the body by means of movable shoulder-blades, which are kept in place by the collar-bone and the strong muscles which over-lay them.

Bones are of various shapes—long, as in the arm and leg ; cuboidal or six-sided, as in the wrist and instep ; and flat, as in the cranium and the shoulder-blades. The larger ones are hollow, which property gives them more strength in proportion to weight than could otherwise have been obtained, and also secures a permanent storehouse for nutriment in the form of marrow, which seems to be set aside as a re-served fund for the sustenance of the body when all other supplies fail.

The connections of the bones, called joints, are very beautiful contrivances, which no mechanic or artist could improve. These connections are of various kinds—by sutures or a sort of dovetailing, by cartilaginous attachments, and by movable joints. There are hinge joints, allowing only a forward and backward movement, and ball and socket joints, which allow the bone to move in all directions.

2. *The Ligaments.*—The ligaments, already incidentally mentioned, help to form the joints, and are properly called organs of connection. Their strength and toughness is so great that it is almost impossible, by means of any ordinary force, to tear them asunder.

"It is wonderful," a distinguished medical writer says, "to see how admirably the ligaments are arranged to answer the purposes for which they are intended! Where the ends of two bones meet, as in some of the joints, ligaments pass across from one to the other; and so firm are they in their structure, that they never allow the joint to become loose, however much it may be exercised. Some of the ligaments are arranged so as to keep the joint from bending the wrong way. The knee joint, which, were it not for its numerous ligaments, would be altogether unfit for the important offices it fulfills, has in it two of these bands, crossing each other like the legs of a saw-horse, in such a manner as to prevent the leg from being carried too far backward or forward; and to guard against dislocations sideways, strong lateral bands are placed on each side of the joint. Not only the large, but the small bones of the body likewise, are bound together in this way as firmly as if secured by clasps of steel.

3. *The Muscles.*—The muscles are simply bundles of red flesh growing together, and more compact toward the extremities, by which they are attached to the bone, and terminating in white tendons or cords. They are, *par excellence*, the organs of motion. It is by means of them that the indwelling mind, telegraphing its mandates through the appropriate nerves, effects any desired movement, by causing a contraction of the fibers of which they are composed, thus drawing the parts to which they are attached toward each other. This contractile power is very great—so great, in fact, that it may even destroy the cohesion of the parts, or tear the tendon from the bone. There are twenty-seven distinct muscles in the human body, divided into two classes—voluntary and involuntary; the former acting in obedience to the will, and the latter independently of it. Those by means of which we move the limbs belong to the first class, and those which keep the heart in motion and carry on the vital processes, while we sleep as well as when we are awake, to the second. They present a great variety of forms, and are of all lengths, from a fourth of an inch, as in some of the muscles of the larynx, to three feet, as in the sartorius or tailor's muscle, which is used in crossing the legs.

The muscular system, in its development and organic condition, is more under control than any other part of the body—a circumstance of no little importance in connection with changes of temperament and human improvement.

II.—THE VITAL OR NUTRITIVE SYSTEM.

The vital or nutritive system consists of three classes of organs, forming a complicated apparatus of *tubes*, which perform the functions of absorption, circulation, and secretion, and, incidentally, of purification. Their principal seat is the trunk of the body, and they exercise a minute peristaltic or pulsating motion. They are designated as—

1. The Lymphatics ;
2. The Blood-vessels ; and
3. The Glands.

1. *The Lymphatics.*—These are small transparent tubes furnished with valves at short intervals, and connected with the ganglia or glands which are distributed over the body, but are most numerous on the sides of the neck, the arm-pits, the groins, and the mesenteric folds of the intestines. Their office is to absorb nutriment and pass it into the circulation. They convey the lymph from every part of the system to the descending *vena cava*, where it mixes with the venous blood returning to the heart. When, through disease or deficiency of food, the supply of nutriment from the ordinary sources is inadequate to the wants of the system, these absorbents take up the fat which has been deposited in the cellular tissues, to be reserved for a time of need, and empty it into the chyle duct, to be thrown into the circulation. This causes the falling away or emaciation observed in the sick or starving. Even the muscles and cellular tissues are thus appropriated, in extreme cases.

These organs, when they open into the intestines

and serve to convey a portion of the nutriment elaborated by the stomach through the thoracic duct to its proper destination, are called lacteals.

2. *The Blood-Vessels.*—The circulation of the blood is effected by means of a system of *tubes*, consisting of the heart, the arteries, and the veins. The center of circulation is the heart, a muscular organ situated in the lower part of the thoracic cavity, between the two folds of the pleura, which form the central partition of the chest. It consists of two parts, a right and a left, in each of which are two cavities, an auricle and a ventricle. In other words, it forms a double force-pump, most ingeniously constructed, with well-fitted valves, which always act perfectly, and never get out of order and never wear out. These pumps send the bright vitalized blood through the arteries to every part of the system, to be taken up by those minuter organs, the capillaries, whose millions of fibers permeate everywhere, and furnish to each organ and part just the supply needed.

To bring the blood back to the heart to be sent to the lungs and revitalized, we have a system of veins, which, commencing in minute capillaries, like little rills, gradually unite and enlarge till they pour their contents, river-like, through two large tubes (one ascending and the other descending), into the right auricle or receptacle of the heart. A muscular contraction sends it into the right ventricle, which, contracting in turn, forces it into the pulmonary artery, and thence into the lungs, where it is purified and changed by contact with the air, and becomes again fitted for its life-bestowing mission.

3. *The Glands.*—The glands, or filters, are the organs which secrete or deposit not only the various substances of which the different organs are composed, but the fat, milk, hair, and other animal products. They are composed of two sets of capillary vessels, the one for the circulation of arterial blood, and the other for secreting their proper materials. The lungs, stomach, intestines, reproductive organs, and especially the liver, are mainly glandular in structure and function, and so far are included in this system.

" The lungs are two conical organs, situated one on each side of the chest, embracing the heart, and separated from each other by a membranous partition, the mediastinum. On the external or thoracic side they are convex, and correspond with the form of the cavity of the chest ; internally they are concave, to receive the convexity of the heart. Superiorily they terminate in a tapering cone, which extends above the level of the first rib, and inferiorily they are broad and concave, and rest upon the convex surface of the diaphragm. Their posterior border is round and broad, the anterior sharp, and marked by one or two deep fissures, and the interior, which surrounds the base, is also sharp. Each lung is divided into two parts by a long and deep fissure, which extends from the posterior surface of the upper part of the organ, downward and forward, to near the anterior angle of its base. The right lung is larger than the left, in consequence of the inclination of the heart to the left side. It is also shorter, from the great convexity of the liver, which presses the diaphragm

upward upon the right side of the chest, consider-
ably above the level of the left. It has three lobes.
The left lung is smaller, has but two lobes, but is
longer than the right."

The lungs present to the view a spongy mass, made
up of air-tubes, air-cells, and blood-vessels, all bound
together by a cellular tissue. Of the air-cells there
are many millions; and the internal surface presented
by the combined air-cells and air-tubes is probably
more than ten times the external surface of the body.
Around each of these minute cells is woven a net-
work of hair-like tubes, through which come and go
the venous and arterial blood. It is through the
coats of these that the air acts upon and vitalizes the
blood, giving it oxygen and receiving carbonic acid
in return.

The liver, which is the largest gland in the body
(weighing about four pounds), extends from the right
to the left hypochondrium, and is situated obliquely
in the abdomen, its convex surface looking upward
and forward, and its concave downward and backward. It is attached by strong ligaments to the diaphragm and other adjacent parts. Its office is to
secrete bile from the blood, which is poured from the
gall-bladder into the duodenum, a few inches below
the stomach.

The stomach is a musculo-membranous organ, the
office of which is to convert the blood into chyme.

The intestines or bowels, the kidneys (whose office
is to separate the urine from the blood), and the
spleen, are included in this system.

III.—THE MENTAL OR NERVOUS SYSTEM.

The mental or nervous system forms the medium of communication between the soul and the external world, and is the instrument through which thought and emotion culminate in action. It consists, structurally, of a series of *globules* bound by membranous investments into fibers of various forms. The chief seat of this system is the head. It admits, like the other systems, of a division of three orders of organs—

1. Organs of Sense ;
2. The Cerebrum ; and
3. The Cerebellum.

1. *The Organs of. Sense.*—The organs through which we receive impressions from external objects —the eye, the ear, etc.—need not be described. They communicate their impressions to the brain by means of special nerves. They all seem to center in the base of the brain.

2. *The Cerebrum.*—The human brain, speaking of it as a whole, is an oval mass filling and fitting the interior of the skull, and consisting of two substances —a gray, ash-colored, or cineritious portion, and a white, fibrous, or medullary portion. It is divided, both in form and in function, into two principal masses, called the cerebrum and the cerebellum. At its base there are two other portions, called the annular protuberance and the medulla oblongata.

The cerebrum is divided longitudinally by the falx, or scythe-shaped process, into two equal hemispheres, and each of these, in its under surface, into three lobes. But the most remarkable feature in the structure of the cerebral globe is its complicated convolu tions, the furrows between which dip down into the brain and are covered by the pia mater, a delicate fibro-vascular membrane, which lies upon the immediate surface of the brain and spinal marrow, bending down into all their furrows or other depressions. By means of these foldings the surface of the brain is greatly increased, and power gained with the utmost economy of space ; for it is a well-ascertained fact, that in proportion to the number and depth of these convolutions, is the power of the brain. "The mind's revolvings," as Wilkinson beautifully expresses it, "are here represented in moving spirals, and the subtile insinuations of thought, whose path lies through all things, issues with power from the form of cerebral screws. They print their shape and make themselves room on the inside of the skull, and are the most irresistible things in the human world."

The cerebrum is the organ of perception, reflection, and all the other essentially human faculties and sentiments.

3. *The Cerebellum.*—The cerebellum is the organ in which lies the nervous center of the procreative function, and it is related intimately to motive impulse and physical life It lies behind and immediately un-

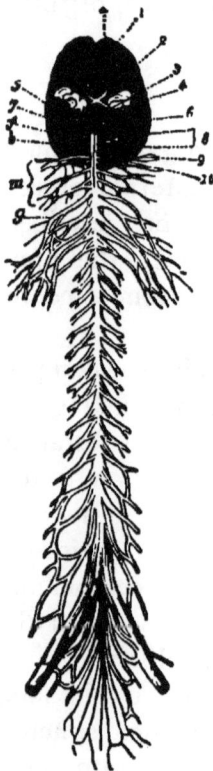

Fig. 1.—Spinal Cord and Nerves.

derneath the cerebrum, and is about one-eighth the size of the latter organ. It is divided into lobes and lobules and consists of a gray and a white substance, like the cerebrum, but differently disposed, the white substance being mainly internal in the latter and external in the former; furthermore, the cerebellum is not convoluted like the cerebrum. There is said to be no direct communication between the lobes of the cerebrum and the cerebellum.

Extending from the base of the brain to the atlas or bony pivot on which the head rests, is the medulla oblongata. It is conical in shape, and may be considered as merely the head or beginning of the spinal cord, which continues it, and extends the brain, as it were, down the vertebral column; and, by means of the nerves which it gives off, and which pass through notches between the vertebræ, connects it with every part of the body.

IV.—OUTLINES OF PHRENOLOGY.

As we shall have frequent occasion, in the following chapters, to make use of phrenological terms and refer to the organs of the mental faculties in the brain, as they may be particularly associated with a given temperamental condition or affected thereby, we have deemed it advisable to insert here such outlines of the science as will at least enable the reader previously ignorant of it (if such readers there be, at this late day) to understand our allusions. We copy, as adapted to our purpose, and as suitable as any sketch we could now prepare, the following sections from

Chapter VII. of "New Physiognomy." No highei authority on this subject than that of the lamented Mr. Wells need be or could be cited.

1. *Phrenology Defined.*—Phrenology is a science and an art. It is the science of the existence, organization, and mode of action of the mind as embodied, and as related through the body to whatever else exists.

The term "Phrenology" means, strictly, Science of the Brain. This term, in itself, relates only to the immediate material organ and instrument of the mind. It is, however, proper enough; for it is the special characteristic of Phrenology to take the brain into the account—to take the common-sense and practical view which looks at the mind, not as it ought to be, nor as it may be claimed that it must be, but as it is. Mind must (to us who are in the flesh) act through a material instrument. Other mental philosophers have not sufficiently considered this, nor the necessary limitations which such an instrument imposes upon mental action, nor the indications derivable from such an instrument about mental action. As these limitations and indications are of the utmost importance, and as their introduction with their right dignity into mental science totally revolutionizes it, and makes it for the first time worthy the name of a science, it is eminently proper that they should characterize the name of the science in its new shape.

2. *Phrenology as an Art.*—Every science has its corresponding art. The principles of science, when modified into application to the practical demands of life, become the rules of their corresponding art.

Phrenology, as an art, consists in judging from the

ncad itself, and from the body in connection with the head, what are the natural tendencies and capabilities of the individual. The practical uses of this art arc many. They consist in applying to the practical needs of life the principles of phrenological science. For instance, it is a principle of Phrenology that, *all other conditions being the same,* the largest brain is the best. In selecting an apprentice, a clerk, therefore, or a lawyer, or a helper, or counselor of any kind, he who practices the art of Phrenology would choose, out of any two or more, him with the largest head, *provided other conditions, such as quality, shape, etc., were equal.* Mistakes would sometimes occur in applying this rule, but in the long run it would be found far more correct than any other known means.

Again, it is the principle of Phrenology that there are separate mental faculties. It is another, that these faculties may be dealt with, trained, or neglected, separately. It is another, that where faculties are defective or feeble, their defect or weakness can usually be made up for by the employment of some other faculty or faculties. It is easy to see that these principles, reduced to rules, would form a very important part of a system of education, particularly of self-education; for evidently an intelligent person, trying one combination of faculties after another, will be able ultimately to exercise himself in exactly such habits of thinking and feeling as will best make up for the points in which he is wanting. If, for instance, he knows that he is deficient in Cautiousness, he can cultivate habits of forethought, reflection, recollection, and observation. This procedure will use Causality.

2

Comparison, Eventuality, and Individuality to do the
work of Cautiousness, and will, at the same time, tend
to stimulate and strengthen the faculty of Cautious‐
ness as a separate instinct.

3. *The Basis of Phrenology.*—The science of Phre‐
nology is based upon observation. Its principles are
simply the recital of truths which lie open before
every man's eye. It is therefore as capable of dem‐
onstration as chemistry or natural philosophy. In
this it differs entirely from all previous systems of
mental science. These have been based upon *a priori*
assumptions (that is, things taken for granted) to be‐
gin with. Having thus the radical imperfections of
mere human conception in their very rudiments and
seeds, they have been muddled, visionary, unpractical,
sophistical, unprogressive, and useless, even almost as
much as the verbal scholastic philosophies of the
Middle Ages.

4. *First Principles.*—Phrenology does not now claim
to be an entirely completed science. As far as it has
now advanced it consists as a science of two parts, viz.:

(1). A system of physiological facts and their cor‐
responding mental phenomena.

(2). A system of mental philosophy deduced from
these facts and phenomena, and from other facts and
phenomena related to them.

The chief principles of the basis or fundamental or
physiological part of the science of Phrenology may
be stated thus:

(1). The brain is the special organ of the mind.
The essence and mode of operation of the mind itself
are inscrutable; we can only study its manifestations

(2). The mind, though essentially a unit, is made up of about forty different faculties, each of which is manifested by means of a particular part of the brain, set apart exclusively for it and called its organ. The faculties may be possessed in different degrees by the same person, and so may the same faculty by different persons.

(3). When other conditions are the same, the larger .he brain the stronger it is; and the larger the portion of brain occupied for the manifestation of a faculty, the stronger its manifestation.

(4). Those portions of brain used for faculties related to each other are located together. Thus the brain is divided into regions or groups, as well as into organs. The location and boundaries of these organs and regions may be best learned from the Phrenological Bust, and the accompanying diagram (fig. 2).

(5). Each group has its collective function. The propelling faculties give force in all actions; the social adapt us to our fellows; the selfish lead us to take care of ourselves; the intellectual enable us to understand men and things, whatever is to be known, and the means of dealing with them; and the moral and religious are meant to control all the rest by subjecting them to the tribunals of kindness, justice, and of the Divine Law.

(6). The original normal conditions which determine the excellence and efficiency of the mind as operative through the brain are:

1. Quantity of brain.
2. Quality of fiber of brain.
3. Relative size of parts of brain.
4. Influence of body upon brain.

(7). Each faculty is susceptible of improvement or
deterioration, and may be strengthened, perverted,
neglected, or weakened.

(8). Each faculty is in itself good, and was given

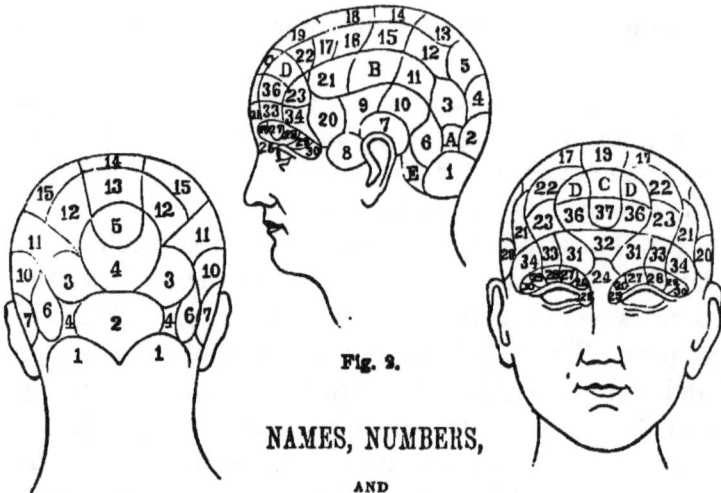

Fig. 2.

NAMES, NUMBERS,

AND

LOCATION OF THE ORGANS.

1. AMATIVENESS.
A. CONJUGAL LOVE.
2. PARENTAL LOVE.
3. FRIENDSHIP.
4. INHABITIVENESS.
5. CONTINUITY.
E. VITATIVENESS.
6. COMBATIVENESS.
7. DESTRUCTIVENESS.
8. ALIMENTIVENESS.
9. ACQUISITIVENESS.
10. SECRETIVENESS.
11. CAUTIOUSNESS.
12. APPROBATIVENESS.

13. SELF-ESTEEM.
14. FIRMNESS.
15. CONSCIENTIOUSNESS.
16. HOPE.
17. SPIRITUALITY.
18. VENERATION.
19. BENEVOLENCE.
20. CONSTRUCTIVENESS.
21. IDEALITY.
B. SUBLIMITY.
22. IMITATION.
23. MIRTH.
24. INDIVIDUALITY.
25. FORM.

26. SIZE.
27. WEIGHT.
28. COLOR.
29. ORDER.
30. CALCULATION.
31. LOCALITY.
32. EVENTUALITY.
33. TIME.
34. TUNE.
35. LANGUAGE.
36. CAUSALITY.
37. COMPARISON.
C. HUMAN NATURE.
D. SAUVITY.

by the Creator for good. The improvement of man,
therefore, does not imply the extinction, or distortion,
or stunting of any faculty, nor the creation of new
ones, but the culture needed by each, the harmoniz-

ing of all, and their pleasant action separately or together, in due subordination, and with the right
degree of activity.

In addition to these diagrams, the student of Phrenology should have at hand a PHRENOLOGICAL BUST,
somewhere near the size of life, showing the exact
location of each organ. Then by comparing living
heads one with another, the differences would appear
most palpable. Extend your observations, and compare the well-known characters of those having long
and narrow heads with those of persons who have
short and broad heads; or compare the high heads
with the low, and however skeptical you may be, you
will be compelled to accept the general principles of
Phrenology.

II.

A GENERAL VIEW OF THE TEMPERAMENTS.

WHEN we compare man with the lower animals, we observe certain characteristic features which do not permit us, for a moment, to confound him with even the most elevated of them. Comparing man with man, while we recognize specific traits common to all individuals of the race, we also note no less obvious differences. One is tall and muscular; another, short and plump; a third, small and slender. This dainty brown-haired girl is delicately fair, we say—the rose and the lily softly blend on her cheek; that boy is as ruddy as a Spitzenberg apple; yonder man is swarthy and has black eyes, while those of the girl are gray and the boy's blue. We also observe that the functions of life are not performed in all with the same degree of force or rapidity, and that their likes and dislikes have neither the same direction nor the same intensity. These differences, with others which need not be here specified, are the results and the indications of what is called Temperament—the *corporis habitus* of the ancients—which may be briefly defined as "a particular state of the constitution depending upon the relative proportion of its different masses and the relative energy of its different functions."

We have shown in the preceding chapter that the

body is made up of certain grand systems of organs with their various subdivisions. First, we have the bony framework, bound together by ligaments, and overlaid with bundles of muscular fibers, by means of which its parts are moved and locomotion produced—the whole constituting the Motive or Mechanical System ; second, the Vital or Nutritive System, whose principal masses lie in the chest and abdomen, and consist of lymphatics, blood-vessels, and glands, performing such functions as digestion, secretion, circulation, and depuration ; and, third, the Mental or Nervous System, having its principal seat in the cranium, but extending itself, in minute ramifications, through every part of the body, and furnishing the mediums of sensation and volition.

It is by the combination of these constitutional elements, in various proportions, that the body is *tempered*— the predominating element determining the *temper*, or Temperament, and the others the innumerable modifications it may present.

It must be evident from this view of the nature of the various states of the constitution, that in their ultimate analysis, the Temperaments must be as numerous as the individuals of the human race—no two persons, probably, having precisely the same physical organization—that is, the same proportion of each elemental ingredient of the compound structure in which each lives, moves, and has a being.

It is essential for practical purposes, therefore, to reduce these numberless individual peculiarities to their simplest elements, and adopt some classification under which we can group together such persons as resemble each other in certain particulars, or who have a similar organization.   To this end, writers on the subject have generally considered the Temperaments under from three to five general heads, each, of course, susceptible of subdivision.

Temperament, as we have said, is a constitutional condition produced by the mixing in various proportions of certain physical elements.   A particular Temperament is the result of the preponderance of one of these elements over all the others, all the elements existing in each case.   In theory we may suppose all of them represented in exactly equal proportions. The ancients, assuming the possibility of such cases, were accustomed to speak of the *Temperamentum Temperatum*—the Temperate, Harmonious, or Balanced Temperament.   We are hardly able to conceive, however, in the human species, a single instance in which there is a perfect equilibrium in all its parts; at the same time, as we do find, in rare instances, persons in whom the different systems of organs are so nearly equal in development, that it is difficult to determine which predominates, and, therefore, sometimes speak of them as having a Balanced Temperament—the best Temperament of all, for the general purposes of existence—and one that will become more and more common as the race progresses in knowledge of its own organization and in the practical application of the laws of life.

I.—THE CAUSES OF TEMPERAMENTAL CONDITIONS.

We are accustomed to speak of Temperament as a cause rather than an effect—a cause of various men-

tal characteristics with which its diverse indications
are found associated; and, in a certain sense, this is a
correct expression of a fact, the conditions of the body
largely affecting the manifestations of the mind; but,
primarily, the constitutional peculiarities of the phys-)
ical system are the effects of pre-existing mental traits, /
either in the subject or his progenitors, and become
causes affecting character, only as they react upon it.

Everywhere it is the indwelling life which determines the organization and external forms of things.
In the seed-germ lies hidden the living principle which
settles beyond the possibility of change the specific
character of the future plant, and even to some extent its less permanent traits, such as size, vigor, and
fruitfulness. In the same way the impregnated animal ovum infolds the unborn organism. Knowing
its parentage, we predict with certainty in advance
its racial characteristics, and with some confidence
its individual peculiarities. The first direction has
already been given to the vital forces, creating a tendency to a certain mental and physical constitution—
the latter as a consequence of the former —and whatever influences may thereafter, either before or after
birth, be brought to bear upon it, this original tendency must always remain a potent element in the
combination.

The brain takes its form and quality from the intelligence which creates and makes use of it, and the
body is modeled after the pattern set by the brain;
so that Temperament is primarily a result and not a
cause of character. The bodily habit is the outgrowth
of a spiritual condition.

2*

As in speaking of the different Temperaments, in detail, we shall have occasion to show what particular causes tend to create and develop each, it is not necessary here to go beyond these general statements; but we must beg the reader to observe that while we wish to impress upon the mind the fact that the temperamental conditions of the body are the results of pre-existing mental characteristics and states, we by no means undervalue the reactive influence of Temperament upon mental characteristics and states. Having to deal mainly with temperamental conditions as we find them already constituted and established, this last view of the matter becomes, in practice, a very important one.

II.—THE ANCIENT DOCTRINE OF THE TEMPERAMENTS.

The ancients did not fail to observe those differences of bodily organization and functional action, with their accompanying mental peculiarities, which we have noted as distinguishing the individuals of the human race, one from another; and four Temperaments, founded on certain constitutional conditions, were recognized and described by Hippocrates, "the father of medicine." These Temperaments, according to his theory, depended upon what were then known as the four primary components of the human body—the blood, the phlegm, the yellow bile, and the black bile. The preponderance of one or the other of these components in a person produces his peculiar constitution or Temperament. Persons in whom the blood predominates, he says, have the Sanguine Temperament; if phlegm be in excess, the Phlegmatic Temperament; if yellow bile be most fully developed, the Choleric Temperament is produced; and if black bile be most abundant, the Melancholic Temperament.

Paulus Ægineta, an ancient physician, adopting the theory and following the classification of Hippocrates, describes these Temperaments as follows:

1. *The Sanguine Temperament.*—The Sanguine or Hot and Moist Temperament is more fleshy than is proper, hairy and hot to the touch. Persons having this Temperament in excess are liable to putrid disorders.

2. *The Phlegmatic Temperament.*—The Phlegmatic or Cold and Moist Temperament is gross, fat, and lax. The skin is soft and white; the hair tawny and not abundant; the limbs and muscles weak; the veins invisible; the character timid, spiritless, and inactive.

3. *The Choleric Temperament.*—The Choleric or Warm and Dry Temperament is known by abundant dark hair; large and prominent veins and arteries; dark skin; and a well-articulated muscular body.

4. *The Melancholic Temperament.*—The Melancholic or Cold and Dry Temperament is known by hard, slender, and white bodies; small muscles and joints; and little hair. In disposition, persons of this Temperament are timid, spiritless, and desponding.

The ancients discovered or fancied certain correspondences between the Temperaments and the various ages, passions, degrees of temperature, climatic conditions, and so on. Thus:

1. The Phlegmatic corresponds with infancy, timidity, spring and a temperate climate;

2. The Sanguine, with youth, emulation, summer and a warm climate;

3. The Choleric with manhood, ambition, autumn and a hot climate;

4. The Melancholic, with age, moroseness, winter and a cold climate.

III.—MODIFICATIONS OF THE ANCIENT DOCTRINE.

The doctrines of Hippocrates and the ancient physicians were often discussed, but never greatly modified, until the advances made in physiology and humoral pathology in comparatively recent times rendered their defects too obvious to be longer overlooked; and even then, the same classification and nomenclature were generally adhered to. Stahl first adapted them to the modern views of physiology and pathology. At a later day, Dr. Gregory, to the four Temperaments of the ancients, added a fifth, which he called the Nervous Temperament, while Cullen reduced them to two—the Sanguine and the Melancholic.

Richerand, who devotes considerable space in his *" Elemens de Physiologie"* to the Temperaments, writes on the subject with much good sense and clearness. He considers the melancholic or Atrabilious Temperament of the ancients as a diseased and abnormal rather than a natural state of the constitution, and the Nervous Temperament of Dr. Gregory as equally so.

The ancients (and the same remark will apply to the greater number of modern writers on the subject) were accustomed to look upon the Temperaments from

a merely physiological or rather a pathological stand-
point, and little, comparatively, was said or known of
the reciprocal influences of physical and mental qualities and states. The Sanguine Temperament—the
happiest of all—however, was believed to give cheerfulness and careless good humor; the Phlegmatic, to
incline its subjects to laziness, sleepiness,.and torpidity;
the Choleric, to dispose men to be precipitate and impetuous, prone to anger, impatience, temerity, and
quarrels; and the Melancholic, to induce timidity,
suspiciousness, inordinate anxiety, and tardiness in
action. "Melancholic men," Hoffmann says, "should
be counselors; choleric persons, generals, ambassadors,
and orators; and sanguinous people, courtiers; but
men who have the misfortune to be phlegmatic must
be condemned to the lowest employments, being fit
only for common laborers or soldiers."

IV.—THE BRAIN AS A TEMPERAMENTAL ELEMENT.

It will be observed that, so far, no account is taken
of the brain as an element entering into the process
of *tempering* the constitution, nor is the nervous system apparently considered, except by Dr. Gregory in
his questionable addition to the list of Temperaments.
The writers quoted and referred to in the preceding
sections, even so far back as Hippocrates, knew all
that was necessary to know, in a merely physiological
point of view, of the lungs, the liver, the heart, and
the stomach, and attributed to them their proper
functions. They were acquainted, also, with the reciprocal action of these organs, and recognized the fact

that upon the proper balance of their forces depends
the health of the body; but the brain was an unex-
plored region—an anatomical *terra incognita*. Dr. Gall,
"the Columbus of the mental world," added its broad
fields to the domains of general knowledge and made
it obvious enough that it must be an important factor
in any problem involving temperamental conditions.
The attention of Dr. Gall and his co-worker, Dr.
Spurzheim, however, was too closely confined to the
brain itself, in its relations with mental manifestations,
to permit them to add much to our knowledge of the
Temperaments. The latter seems to have adopted
the modification of the ancient system proposed by
Dr. Gregory, so far as the Nervous Temperament is
concerned. He briefly describes four Temperaments,
as follows:

V.—Dr. Spurzheim's Description of the Temperaments.

1. *The Lymphatic Temperament.*—The Lymphatic
or Phlegmatic Temperament is indicated by a pale
white skin, fair hair, roundness of form, and repletion
of the cellular tissue. The flesh is soft, the vital actions
are languid, the pulse is feeble; all indicate slowness
and weakness in the vegetative, affective, and intellectual functions.

2. *The Sanguine Temperament.* — The Sanguine
Temperament is proclaimed by a tolerable consistency
of flesh, moderate plumpness of parts, light or chestnut hair, blue eyes, great activity of the arterial system, a strong, full, and frequent pulse, and an animated
countenance. Persons thus constituted are easily af-

fected by external impressions, and possess greater energy than those of the former temperament.

3. *The Bilious Temperament.*—The Bilious Temperament is characterized by black hair, a dark, yellowish, or brown skin, black eyes; moderately full, but firm muscles, and harshly-expressed forms. Those endowed with this constitution have a strongly-marked and decided expression of countenance; they manifest great general activity and functional energy.

4. *The Nervous Temperament.*—The external signs of the Nervous Temperament are fine thin hair, delicate health, general emaciation, and smallness of the muscles, rapidity in the muscular actions, vivacity in the sensations. The nervous system of individuals so constituted preponderates extremely and they exhibit great nervous sensibility.

This and similar modifications of the ancient system are still received by medical and physiological writers generally.

VI.—NORMAL TEMPERAMENTAL CONDITIONS.

It remained for the later Phrenologists to eliminate from the old systems all the abnormal conditions and place the doctrine of the Temperaments on a strictly anatomical and physiological basis. Adopting the simple classification of the bodily organs set forth in our first chapter, including them all under the three heads of—

1. The Motive or Mechanical System;
2. The Vital or Nutritive System; and
3. The Mental or Nervous System;—

and considering simply the healthful and normal ac-

tion of these diverse orders of organs, as they affect
character and are affected by it, they found in each
the basis for a Temperament, the three including,
in their various combinations, all possible constitutional conditions. Adopting the nomenclature of
anatomy rather than that of pathology, they called
them—

1. The Motive Temperament;
2. The Vital Temperament; and
3. The Mental Temperament.

" Each of these temperaments is determined by the
predominance of the class of organs from which it
takes its name. The first is marked by a superior development of the osseous and muscular systems, forming the locomotive apparatus; in the second the vital
organs, the principal seat of which is in the trunk,
give the tone to the organization; while in the third
the brain and nervous system exert the controlling
power."

As we purpose to make this simple and comprehensive system the principal basis of our practical teach-
ings in this work, availing ourself, as occasion requires,
however, of the advantages of what may be called the
pathological system of previous writers, we shall reserve for separate chapters full expositions of both.
Our object here has been simply to prepare the reader,
by a general view, for the better comprehension of
the details which are to follow.

III.

THE PATHOLOGICAL VIEW OF THE TEMPERAMENTS.

WITH very few exceptions, writers on the Temperaments, from Hippocrates to Thomas, have been physicians. In the study and practice of their profession, these gentlemen are accustomed to have their attention constantly directed to the various diseases and abnormal conditions of the constitution, and it is not strange that they have taken account of these conditions, as well as of its healthful and normal states, in their classifications, or that they have adopted, in their nomenclature, the terms of pathology rather than those of physiology and anatomy; nor are we disposed to quarrel with them or to depreciate their labors on this account. Their system has a solid foundation and a real value. The stomach, the lungs, the liver, and the brain furnish four distinct constitutional influences, either of which predominating, gives its peculiar conformation and complexion to the body, and its specific tone to the mind.

The Temperaments thus formed may all represent perfectly normal bodily conditions, but two of them —the Lymphatic and the Nervous—as generally described, are evidently the results of abnormal or diseased action. We accept them as such. They are not any the less real from being aberrant or unnatural. Such states of the constitution are far too common to

be ignored, and whether we call them Temperaments
or give them other names, it is necessary to take them
into account, not only in treating disease, but in estimating character, educating children, or choosing a
profession or a companion.

There need be no conflict between this system and
the simpler and more natural one to which we have
given preference in this work. All that is necessary
in applying the two conjointly, is to bear in mind the
distinction between the normal and the abnormal activities of the organs of the body and the brain.

We adopt, then, in this chapter, the classification
and nomenclature now most generally accepted and
made use of by medico-physiological writers, and de-
scribe in detail the four Temperaments known as—

1. The Lymphatic Temperament;
2. The Sanguine Temperament;
3. The Bilious Temperament; and
4. The Nervous Temperament.

I.—THE LYMPHATIC TEMPERAMENT (Fig. 3).

This is essentially the Phlegmatic Temperament
of the ancients, and is based, as its name indicates,
upon the predominance of the lymphatic system, the
office of which is to convey the lymph from all parts
of the body toward the heart. The undue preponderance of these organs, and of the stomach and the
glandular system, with which they are in close relation, leads to an excessive secretion of the watery
fluids of the body, resulting in repletion, a sluggish
circulation, and a general clogging of the vital machin-

LOUIS XVIII.

JACK HENDERSON.   HON. WM. MAULE PANMURE, M. P.

FIG. 3.—THE LYMPHATIC TEMPERAMENT.

There is great difficulty in securing portraits representing this Temperament, but
the above shows its general tendency.

PLATE I.

ery. The muscles, burdened with a useless load, act with difficulty and lack promptness in their movements; the heart beats slowly; and the brain, receiving tardily an inadequate supply of vitalized blood, partakes of the sluggishness of the general system.

1. *Causes.*—During the first months of life, the function of nutrition takes precedence of all others. In infancy, therefore, those organs on which nutrition specially depends—the stomach and the other glandular organs closely connected therewith, and the lymphatics—naturally exercise a predominating influence. There is manifested, at this period, in many cases, an inherited predisposition to an excessive development of the lymphatic system, which, if not counteracted, necessarily results in abnormal conditions of the constitution, most unfavorable to health and mental power. It is exceedingly important, therefore, that the causes which are calculated to aggravate this tendency should be known, in order that they may be avoided and the necessary counteracting influences be brought to bear, while the subject is still plastic and easily affected by them.

The causes most influential in producing that abnormal constitutional condition known as the Lymphatic Temperament are such as affect the subject not only directly in his own person, but pre-natally, through its progenitors. They are both physical and mental. Among the former are:

(1). Living in low, moist, or marshy districts pervaded by malaria. Holland, Belgium, England, and parts of the Southern States of the American Union furnish many striking examples.

(2). Residing in densely-shaded places, where the sun penetrates but little and the air is confined and therefore not easily purified. Confinement within doors, in rooms kept constantly darkened by blinds and curtains, is another form of the same potent evil—exclusion of sunlight and fresh air.

(3). The crowding together of many people, as in the tenement-houses of cities, resulting in a poisoned atmosphere and general filthiness.

(4). Sedentary in-door employments and lack of exercise in the open air.

(5). Errors of diet, especially in connection with the other causes enumerated, and where there is a pre-existing tendency to the lymphatic habit. A too exclusive use of watery vegetables, leguminous seeds, and dishes prepared with milk is found very injurious in such cases. In children manifesting the unfavorable predisposition referred to, the too long-continued use of a milk diet will be likely to greatly aggravate it.

The mental causes of this temperamental condition, though perhaps less obvious, are equally powerful. They are numerous, but the most noteworthy are:

(1). A false system of education, calculated to develop the mind at the expense of the body, repress the natural activities of childhood and youth, and prevent the harmonious expansion of the faculties, and thus lower the tone of every part of the general system.

(2). An utter neglect of mental culture, equally injurious to the abuse of intellectual development referred to in the preceding paragraph, leaving the mind in a half-dormant state and fostering idleness, indolence, indifference, and *ennui.*

(3). Care, anxiety, disappointment, grief, and the depressing passions generally, which impair the brain and debilitate and soften the body and prevent its proper development.

These and other similar influences, mental and physical, tend to create and develop not only a most undesirable constitutional condition, but often lead to the establishment of a scrofulous habit of body, almost sure to culminate in confirmed disease.

2. *Characteristics.*—(1). Physically, persons in whom the Lymphatic Temperament is strongly developed are characterized by a stature above rather than below the medium, except in those cases in which excessive morbid conditions in childhood and youth have led to an arrest of development; fullness of body, sometimes amounting to excessive corpulence, caused rather by the settling of the watery fluids under the skin than by the bulk of the muscles; softness and flabbiness of flesh; contours, full, but without grace or beauty; articulations, voluminous, but badly formed; extremities, large and ugly; features, full, heavy, and expressionless, the cheeks being often pendant and the lips thick; skin, a dull leaden white, faded or yellowish and generally cold and moist; hair, fine, silky, but lustreless, a pale blonde, sometimes reddish—in childhood, sometimes a dull white; expression, mild, benevolent, timid, often sad; voice, monotonous; pulse, slow and feeble; movements, sluggish; walk, slow, painful and uncertain. In ex-

treme cases, some of these characteristics are enormously exaggerated. In women, the greater comparative fullness and activity of the lacteals give them more influence in the lymphatic system, and modify favorably the manifestations of this Temperament.

(2). The mental characteristics of the Lymphatic Temperament are in unison with the bodily traits we have described. The brain is not less sluggish than the body, and there is a strong desire for repose, and an aversion, more or less invincible, to everything which calls for active exertion. There is often excellent common sense, good judgment, and fine general abilities, though little originality or imagination; but these qualities are generally of little value to their possessor, on account of the constitutional inertness which prevents their efficient exercise. The disposition is mild, amiable, and timid, with a tendency to sadness, indifference, and *ennui.* The currents of life are too sluggish to give any useful motion to the mental machinery.

3. *Remedial Agencies.*—To correct the grave and deeply-seated evils of which the Lymphatic Temperament is an indication, is certainly difficult, especially when they are congenital or have become chronic; but, except in extreme cases, we need not despair of effecting an improvement, if not a radical cure. Among the most important and generally available means to this end are :

(1). The removal, so far as possible, of the causes which have been instrumental in producing the objectionable condition, whether these be physical or mental—a residence in an insalubrious district, unhealthful surroundings, a bad diet, a false educational system, or depressing passional influences.

(2). The direct application of counteracting agencies, such as a nutritious, strengthening, and somewhat stimulating diet, consisting largely of wholesome animal food; such outdoor exercises as will best promote the development of the muscular and vital systems; and such mental stimuli as are calculated to awaken the dormant energies of the mind. An interest in any study, occupation, or pursuit once excited, and an important step in the right direction has been gained, making the succeeding ones comparatively easy. The conditions against which we have to contend are negative ones—torpidity, stagnation, inertia. We must, then, stimulate, encourage, vitalize—promote activity in body and brain.

II.—THE SANGUINE TEMPERAMENT (Fig. 4).

The predominance of the arterial circulatory system, the lungs and the capillary vessels generally, constitute the organic basis of the Sanguine Temperament—the most favored of all in those desirable physical conditions conducive to health and happiness, without, however, promising so much in the way of an illustrious or useful career. As now constituted and described, it is a modification of the Sanguine Temperament of the ancients, the changes being the results of modern researches in physiology and pathology.

1. *Causes.*—This Temperament, being a positive rather than a negative constitutional condition, and replete with vigor and healthful activities, tends

strongly to perpetuate itself. When fully developed in either parent, it very generally forms a strong if not a controlling element in the progeny. Of the causes which promote its development, the following are the most important :

(1). A climate neither too moist nor too dry, and free from malaria, and a healthful habitation and surroundings, admitting the sunlight, and insuring at all times an abundance of fresh air.

(2). Daily, active outdoor exercise, embracing sports and employments calculated to interest the mind as well as invigorate the body.

(3). A wholesome diet, in which foods selected from the animal kingdom hold an important place, and into which watery vegetables, strong acids, and milk do not enter too largely.

(4). A rational system of education, in which, in its earlier stages at least, more prominence is given to health and physical development than to mental culture, and which is free from those injurious restraints and that repressive discipline which prevent the child or the youth from enjoying without disobedience or a sense of wrong-doing the sports of his age.

(5). The culture and development of the affections and the removal of the causes of the violent passions of ambition, envy, jealousy, and hate, which exert an exhausting and depressing influence.

2. *Characteristics.*—(1). The Sanguine Temperament is characterized, physically, by a stature generally above the medium ; a well-proportioned body, the chest being particularly well-developed, and the

B. GRATZ BROWN.

FIG. 4.—THE SANGUINE TEMPERAMENT.

PLATE II.

muscles modeled for elegance and suppleness rather
than for power and solidity; articulations thin, slender, and in harmony with the members, the extremities of which they unite, and with the general habit
of the body, which indicates activity and grace rather
than strength, its type being the Apollo Belvedere.
The head is generally well formed and moderate in
size, and the proportions between the cranium and
the face harmonious. The skin is fine, soft, pliable,
and transparent; the complexion, suffused by the
highly-vitalized blood which the powerful arterial
system supplies, always fresh and ruddy; the hair,
blonde, red or chestnut, rarely dark, and the expression cheerful, frank, benevolent, and sincere. The
face is inclined to roundness, the lips are full and red,
and the eyes blue, brilliant, and expressive. The
pose of the body is natural and dignified, and the
movements graceful, easy, and precise. The organization, as a whole, is characterized by vigor, warmth,
and functional activity.

(2). As the physical functions are rapidly and vigor-
ously performed and the blood rich and warm, so are
the mental processes characterized by facility and
quickness, and the disposition by ardor and impulsiveness. Ready, facile perceptions, brilliant imagination,
great versatility and vivacity of expression, accompanied by an inability to fix the attention long upon
any one subject, give to the judgment more promptness than solidity, and to aquisition and performance
more variety and showiness than depth and originality.
A man of this Temperament attains more success in
the drawing-room among women than among serious-

3

ly-minded men, and more distinction on the tribune, in literary labor and in the fine arts, than in the culture of abstract or positive science, or in studies necessarily requiring close and long-continued attention. Of the powerful and sustained efforts of the highest genius he is utterly incapable. These intellectual traits are supplemented by a cheerful, lively, easy disposition, great good nature, kindness, credulity, and candor. There is always a great fondness for good living, pleasant companionship, and the light and trifling rather than the serious affairs of life. In their affections, persons of this Temperament are ardent, but often inconstant, and their plans and opinions are liable to sudden changes. Naturally impatient and fiery, they are often thrown into violent passions, but their outbursts are almost always followed by returning kindness, and they are seldom obdurate or revengeful. Their strong appetites, their active social affections, their impatience of restraint and love of excitement and change, often lead them, when not restrained by well-established moral principles, into a course of frivolity and dissipation. Avoiding this, they generally lead a cheerful if not a jovial life, enjoying the present, forgetting the past, and concerning themselves little with the future.

3. *Cultivation.*—Where the sanguine element of the constitution is deficient, every effort should be made, by means of judicious cultivation, to increase its development. The agencies to be made use of will suggest themselves on recalling the causes which lead to its predominance, set forth at the commencement of this section. They consist—

(1). Negatively, in the avoidance of sedentary employments; confinement in close, darkened, or shaded rooms; a low, innutritious diet; continuous and excessive mental application; too much muscular exercise; all depressing emotions, and everything calculated to lower the tone of the system ; and—

(2). Positively, in an exposure, as constant as practicable, to fresh air and sunshine ; active employments and recreations; persistent systematic exercises tending to expand the chest and increase the power of the heart and lungs; a strong, nutritious, mixed diet; sufficient intellectual exertion to employ and direct the mind, without fatiguing it ; cheerful companionship and pleasant surroundings; and, if possible, the full satisfaction of the social affections.

4. *Counteractive Agencies.*—Even a constitutional condition, natural and eminently healthful in its typical form, may, when in excess, become the source of grave evils, or its characteristic tendencies may lead to hurtful indulgences, unless restrained by the modifying influences of the other temperamental elements, or by a predominating sense of moral responsibility. We must, therefore, learn, if possible, how to counteract as well as to encourage, strengthen, and develop these tendencies. In the case of the Sanguine Temperament, the counteracting agencies to be brought into play are these:

(1). Increased activity (leading to increased development) of the muscular and the nervous systems, through such exercise and culture as may be best calculated to call out their strength and give them more influence in the organization. A close, patient application (within the limits of health) to some scientific study, or a steady adherence to a regular course of severe muscular exercise, will effect wonders in bringing the system into harmony.

(2). The awakening and development of the moral sentiments, and especially those imparting a sense of right and wrong, self-respect, and human responsibility. These will tend to turn the irrepressible activities of this Temperament into channels of innocent and honorable recreation and work, and prevent its strong and sudden impulses from carrying it into the excesses of folly and vice.

III.—THE BILIOUS TEMPERAMENT (Fig. 5).

The Bilious Temperament pivots on the liver, the predominating influence of which, through its proper functional operations, together with those of the nervo-ganglionic centers closely connected therewith, constitutes its physical basis, though it involves, to a great extent, the whole nutritive system, and especially the digestive apparatus.

Causes.—Aside from an inherited predisposition to it, which is the most potent cause of this constitutional condition, it may be created and is always fostered and augmented by—

(1). Residence in regions having a dry, hot climate ;

(2). A diet largely composed of animal food, and especially of bacon and other salted, smoked, or spiced meats; tea, coffee, and other stimulating beverages ;

(3). Sedentary habits and lack of sufficient exercise in the open air; .

(4). Violent and unpleasant mental excitements,

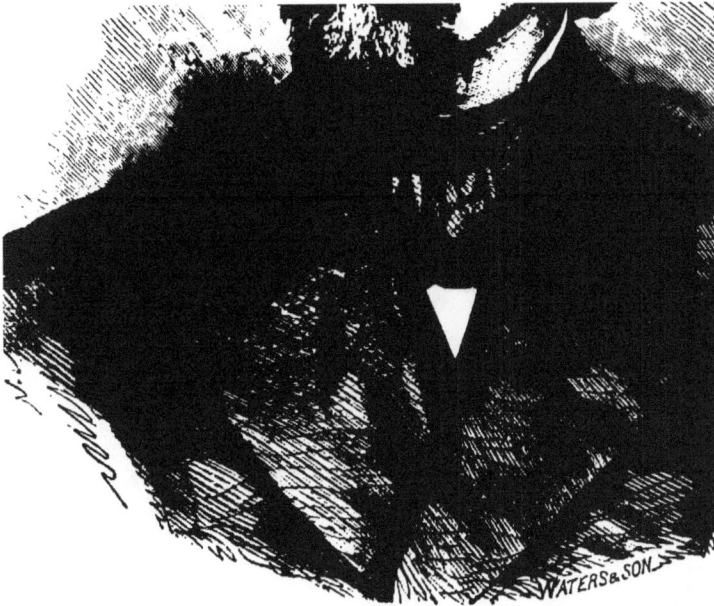

E. H. DIXON, M. D.

FIG. 5.—THE BILLIOUS TEMPERAMENT.

PLATE III.

embittering political contests, revolutionary agitations, religious controversies, and violent passions,
such as envy, jealousy, and hate.

Characteristics.—(1). The Bilious Temperament is
characterized, physically, by a medium stature; a
somewhat angular configuration; strongly-defined
muscular developments; a firm pose; a lofty if not
audacious bearing; abrupt, energetic, and expressive
gestures; a measured walk; and an expression of
countenance generally serious and sometimes somber
and severe. The skin is rather coarse and dry; the
complexion olive, tawny, or dull; the eyes black or
brown, and the hair dark—often black—strong and
abundant. The preponderance of the venous over
the arterial system, places this Temperament in direct
antagonism to the Sanguine, and the excess of bile
sometimes secreted renders the system liable to irritable conditions and bilious diseases.

(2). The mental manifestations of this constitutional condition are all energetically expressed and
unmistakable; and it furnishes generally the most remarkable developments of intellect and passion, the
former rising far above mere cleverness and imagination, into the regions of genius, and the latter often culminating in the sublimest virtues or the most atrocious
crimes. It is characterized by precision of judgment,
power of reasoning, and profundity of perceptions,
rather than by brilliancy and ingeniousness of conceptions. There is a serious earnestness in all its manifestations; a predilection for grave and useful labors;
a distaste for all frivolous pursuits, and a ready renun-
ciation, at need, of amusement and recreation. Un

flinching resolution, dauntless courage, indomitable
perseverance, and a capability for sustained attention
and deep research are equally noteworthy traits.   The
style is rapid, concise, expressive, burning; the elocution measured and calm in ordinary conversation, but
abrupt, incisive, and terrible when expressing violent
emotions.   In its passional or emotional manifestations, this Temperament presents strange contrasts
and contradictions—on the one hand moral grandeur,
generosity, self-sacrifice, heroic devotion; on the other,
ambition, jealousy, envy, vindictive hate, perfidy, and
cruelty.   It is here that the domination of reason and
the moral sentiments over the passions is most necessary, and at the same time most difficult to maintain.
Abandoned to mere impulse, men of this constitution
become insupportably disagreeable.   If conscious of
their defects and errors, they seem proud rather than
ashamed of them, make enemies without number, and,
finally, become isolated, misanthropic, and tired of
existence.   On the contrary, if strongly controlled
and rightly directed, the powerful forces of these vol-
canic natures become beneficent agencies for the ac-
complishment of great ends, overcoming obstacles
which seem to all others insurmountable, and modifying the political and moral condition of the world.
Where the control is imperfect, good and evil are
strangely mingled in the stormy career of such
natures, as illustrated by such historic personages as
Mohammed, Cromwell, and Napoleon.

An excess of the bilious element, resulting in an
irritable condition of the digestive and nervo-ganglionic organs; depressing passions, bitter opposition,

persecution, injustice, the constant wounding of self-love, grief, sad companions, and gloomy surroundings, in connection, frequently, with an indulgence in perverse and immoral inclinations, subversive of both bodily health and mental soundness, lead to that abnormal condition called by the ancients the Melancholic Temperament, in which there is a sickly condition of body; a cold, humid skin; a sallow, discolored complexion; a timid, sorrowful, and languid expression of countenance; a depraved appetite; a painful digestion; disturbed sleep; depression of spirits, defying all consolation; utter discouragement; inability to take things at their natural value, but a setting aside of the real appreciation, in favor of the hallucination of a diseased imagination; the exaggeration of all painful impressions and the lessening of all those which might become agreeable; an irritability which is prone to take offense where none is meant; and a disposition to brood over fictitious wrongs and imaginary misfortunes.

3. *Cultivation.*—The liver, being remote from the brain and more secluded than the organs of circulation from atmospheric and other external influences, the temperamental condition of which it is the source, is less readily affected by direct agencies than those which depend upon more accessible parts and more sensitive tissues. It is, however, to some extent, within our control and may be promoted by judicious cultivation. The means to this end are:

(1). Change of residence to a hotter and drier climate; a diet embracing a larger proportion of animal food; the very moderate use of tea and coffee.

(2). Active participation in the more stirring movements of the day, with the discussions, controversies,
contests, and excitements involved; and the exercise
of all the positive, executive, and aggressive elements
of character.

4. *Counteractive Agencies.*—As there is a direct antagonism between the bilious and the sanguine elements of the constitution, we can always make use
of the one to counteract or modify the other. When,
therefore, there may be an excessive development of
the Bilious Temperament, the most efficient means
of moderating its action, and finally diminishing its
volume and influence, is by increasing the weight of
the adverse or sanguinous element, the means of
doing which have already been set forth under their
proper head.

5. *Controlling Influences.*—The terrible power for
evil as well as for good residing in this Temperament, renders it most important that we should be
able to turn its energies into the right channels and
make them minister to the good of the race. The
moral sentiments must, therefore, be awakened into
healthy activity and the reasoning powers be well
developed by judicious exercise.

6. *Remedial Measures.*—In the case of such abnormal manifestations as those noted as being
characteristic of what is called the Melancholic Temperament, active hygienic measures directed to the
restoration of the general health should be at once
resorted to.

(1). A removal, so far as possible, of all the causes
calculated to aggravate the diseased condition, such

as the use of alcoholic liquors, tea, coffee, salted and smoked meats, spices and condiments, dull or gloomy companionship, and somber or otherwise disagreeable surroundings ;

(2). A carefully selected, cooling, unstimulating diet composed of farinaceous substances, fruits and vegetables ;

(3). Frequent bathing (the Turkish Bath being used, if possible), and constant and systematic outdoor exercise ; and

(4). Pleasant surroundings, cheerful companionship, rational amusements, and constant, but not fatiguing occupation for body and mind.

IV.—THE NERVOUS TEMPERAMENT (Fig. 6).

The abnormal constitutional condition described under this name by medico-physiological writers, is unfortunately sufficiently common in this age and country to be readily recognized. Its pathological character is also evident enough, no healthy man or woman ever presenting the characteristics by which it is distinguished. It consists in the excessive development and morbid activity of the nervous system, including the brain, though the latter organ, taken alone, is not always necessarily either large or particularly influential, the nervo-ganglionic system being often the chief seat of this constitutional condition.

1. *Causes.*—The causes of this temperamental condition are mainly peculiar to our "advanced civilization," in regard to which we are accustomed to boast,

3*

and consist in the training, habits, and modes of life
which this civilization permits and encourages. We
note, as prominent among them :

(1). The hereditary transmission of the constitution of the parents, and the pre-natal influences
brought to bear upon the child during gestation,
through the nervous excitements to which the mother
is often subjected, and which are readily communi-
cated and profoundly affect its organization. These
and similar considerations serve to account for the
frequency of this condition in countries where civilization has assumed an effeminate and luxurious
phase.

(2). A false and pernicious system of infantile nur-
ture, calculated to soften, weaken, and blanch the
tender, young subject, rather than to build up a solid
structure of healthy bone and muscle and transfuse
it with warm, red, vitalized blood. The excessive
precautions taken to secure the infant against cold
and all external atmospheric influences, only foster
and increase the unfavorable hereditary tendencies
noted in the preceding paragraph, and unfit it for the
equally inconsiderate, not to say criminal, exposure
to which, a little later, its tender limbs will be ex-
posed in its sleeveless short dresses.

(3). In early youth, before either body or brain
have attained sufficient consistency and strength to
bear the strain, and while growth and physical training should be the principal objects, commences the
confinement of the school-room with its premature
and excessive intellectual culture—or the word-stuff-
ing which passes for culture—and the sad work, com-

WM. ELLERY CHANNING, D.D.

FIG. 6.—THE NERVOUS TEMPERAMENT.

PLATE IV.

menced before birth and well advanced in infancy, is carried another long step forward. The result is either a breaking down, at this stage, of the general health, followed by an early death, or an intellectual precocity, inadequately sustained by vital stamina, and surely leading to painful disappointments in regard to a career in life, the brilliant promises of which are never sustained.

(4). In mature life, in addition to confinement within doors and lack of exercise, come, if possible, still more serious abuses in the excessive use of tea, coffee, tobacco, and strong liquors; the constant excitements of society; a passionate devotion to pursuits and pleasures calculated to weaken the nerves, while exalting the sensibilities, already too active; and, on the part of some, the cares and anxieties of business. These baleful influences are most prevalent in cities and towns. but, unfortunately, are not confined to them.

2. *Characteristics.*—(1). Among the physical indications of the Nervous Temperament, we find, generally, a stature below the medium; a slight frame; habitual emaciation and a marked predominance of the nervous over the muscular system. The head is generally relatively large and there is a more or less marked disproportion between the cranium and the face. The skin and hair are fine and soft; the eyes often gray and very brilliant; the complexion pale and sometimes sallow; the movements rapid and often irregular or convulsive; and the expression intelligent and vivacious.

(2). All the mental manifestations are generally

lively, prompt, and facile, though sometimes weak
and indecisive.   There is often excessive sensibility, leading sometimes to the most painful emotions;
quick perceptions; brilliant imagination; versatility,
wit, refinement, and taste.   The judgment is seldom trustworthy, and the affections are often inconstant, factitious, and sickly rather than firm,
hearty, and real.   There is little capacity for continued attention to any particular subject or for
patient study or profound research.   Grave discussions, fatigue, and grand abstractions confuse and
overwhelm the mind.   A desire for novelty and
change; an equal facility to learn and to forget; the
love of the world, its superficial distinctions, its futile
pleasures, and its enervating fatigues; absurd sensitiveness; easily wounded self-love; impressions utterly disproportionate, seemingly, to the objects
which produce them, and generally exaggerated views
and feelings are among the irregular characteristics
of the Nervous Temperament, which is most common
among women of the wealthier classes, men devoted
to sedentary pursuits, or to idleness and sensuality,
and to those of both sexes who habitually make
excessive use of tea, coffee, tobacco, and alcoholic
liquors.   It is confined almost exclusively to highly
civilized nations and to warm and temperate climates.

3. *Remedial Measures.*—The abnormal condition
we have described, when fully developed.and chronic,
is very difficult to counteract and overcome, more
particularly on account of the difficulty of removing
all the causes which have led to its firm establish-

ment, and must, so long as they exist, continue to foster it.

(1). We must, however, make it our first object to give the patient, so far as possible, immunity from all the pernicious influences enumerated among the causes of the diseased condition, not forgetting tea, coffee, tobacco, and alcoholic liquors;

(2). Constant exercise, moderate at first, and increased with the increase of strength; daily bathing; tepid in the beginning and administered with caution, but finally colder, for a tonic effect; a nutritious diet, from which strong condiments, and foods not easy of digestion are excluded, must be insisted upon; also,

(3). Occupations and amusements suited to employ healthfully the mind and furnish exercise for the muscles, without exciting the one or fatiguing the other.

IV.

As has been shown in Chapter I., the human body is made up of three grand classes or systems of organs, each of which, as a system, has its special function in the general economy. We have denominated them—

1. The Motive or Mechanical System;
2. The Vital or Nutritive System; and
3. The Mental or Nervous System.

On this natural anatomical basis rests the most simple and satisfactory doctrine of the Temperaments, of which there are primarily three, corresponding with the three systems of organs just named. They are called—

1. The Motive Temperament;
2. The Vital Temperament; and
3. The Mental Temperament.

Each of these Temperaments is determined by the predominance of the class of organs from which it takes its name, the constitution being *tempered* by the admixture of the other elements in a less proportion, all being necessarily present in every human being. The first is marked by a superior development of the osseous and muscular systems forming the locomotive apparatus; in the second, the vital organs, the principle seat of which is the trunk, give the tone to the organization; while in the third the brain and nervous system exert the controlling power. It will

(62)

be observed that this classification differs from the old
or pathological one, principally (aside from its nomenclature) in making the vital or nutritive system the
basis for a single Temperament instead of three. The
heart, lungs, stomach, and abdominal organs all work
harmoniously together, and are too closely connected
to be judiciously separated in considering general
temperamental condition ; but when a closer analysis
becomes necessary, we note the proportional development of the sanguine, the bilious, and the lymphatic elements, the first and third of which are associated more particularly with the Vital Temperament ;
and the second, the condensing and hardening element, affects more generally the Motive Temperament. The Mental Temperament of this classification
corresponds with the Nervous Temperament of the
old system, except that it recognizes only healthy
conditions of the organs on which it depends for its
manifestations.

In the order of their influence, among civilized
peoples, the Mental Temperament stands first and the
Vital next, but we have thought it best to begin, as
in our anatomical description, with the solid basis of
the whole—the bony framework and the temperamental condition resting upon it.

I.—THE MOTIVE TEMPERAMENT (Fig. 7).

The bony framework of the body determines its
general configuration, which is modified, in its details,
by the muscular fibers and cellular tissues which over-
lay it. It is in this framework, which is at the same
time a most wonderful locomotive apparatus, that we

find the physical basis for that constitutional condi
tion called the Motive Temperament. The appropri‑
ateness of the name will be conceded when it is con‑
sidered that not only the ability for action, physical
power, and mental energy, but a love of movement,
a fitness for hard work, and an earnestness of purpose
which ignores ease and needless repose, are among its
characteristics.

    1. *Causes.*—This Temperament is generally hered‑
itary and is the result of climate, topographical con‑
ditions, and habits of life, acting for generations upon
families and nations. Among the most influential
of the physical causes which lead to its existence and
promote its increase, are:

    (1). A dry, stimulating atmosphere, encouraging
physical action and inducing mental vigor, without
disposing one to the confinement of close study;

    (2). Residence in rocky, hilly, and mountainous re‑
gions, where great muscular exertion is required to
gain a subsistence, and where the roads and foot‑
paths are steep and difficult;

    (3). Occupations which tend to develop bone and
muscle rather than cellular tissue or brain, without
dwarfing the latter by inaction, overwork, or repres‑
sion; and

    (4). A diet rich in lime, phosphoric acid, and the
other bone-forming element, as well as in the mate‑
rials for building up the muscular sheathing of the
bones.

    Mental causes affect less obviously this tempera‑
mental condition, but they are by no means without
their influence.

BARON VON LEIBIG.

FIG. 7. THE MOTIVE TEMPERAMENT.

PLATE V.

(1). Whatever hardens the heart, embitters the life, arouses the more violent passions, or gives full play to ambition and the love of power, promotes, through the mental organization, the physical conditions of the Motive Temperament. Political agitations, revolutionary movements, heated religious controversies, opposition in all forms, constant resistance to authority or the will of others, and the necessity for being always watchful and on the defensive, are among the strongest of these influences; to which may be added:

(2). The exercise of authority, especially in military forms, and the weight of great responsibilities, calling for the exercise of the executive faculties to their full capacity, which are also favorable to its culture.

2. *Characteristics.*—(1). Bones proportionally large, and long rather than broad; strong, hard muscles, and prominent articulations, give to the outlines of the form in the Motive Temperament a tendency to angularity and sharpness. The figure is commonly tall and striking, if not elegant; the chest moderate in size and fullness; the shoulders broad and definite; the abdomen proportional; the limbs long and only moderately tapering. The face is oblong; the cheek bones rather high (as in Figs. 8 and 9); the front teeth large; and the features generally prominent and sharply defined. The expression of the countenance is striking, grave, earnest, determined, and sometimes severe and stern.

In reference to color, we find two distinct varieties of this Temperament—the dark and the light, or the

melanchomous and the *xanthous*. In the first the
bilious element is strongly predominant; in the second
the sanguine is sufficiently powerful to impart
its characteristic redness without producing that constitutional condition we recognize as the Vital Temperament. In the dark type, the complexion is
swarthy, brown or olive, the eyes black or brown, and
the hair generally black, strong, and abundant. In
the sanguine type, the complexion may be florid and
the eyes blue, gray, or hazel. The hair is often red
and not infrequently sandy. This variety of the Motive
Temperament is exemplified in the Scandinavian
peoples—Danes, Swedes, and Norwegians—in the
Irishmen of the North, in the Highland Scotch of
the higher class (mainly of Norse origin), and in
many individuals in all Caucasian nations. The dark
or bilious type is most common among Americans,
the tendency of our climate being to produce the
melanic constitution.

Wherever we deem it desirable to distinguish these
two varieties of the Motive Temperament, we shall
designate the first or dark type as the Bilious-Motive,
and the second or light variety as the Sanguine-
Motive. If this mixing up of the old and new no-
menclatures be considered objectionable, they may
be called the Melano-Motive and the Xantho-Motive,
respectively, or simply the Dark-Motive and the
Light-Motive.

In persons of this Temperament, firmness of texture characterizes all the organs, imparting great
strength and endurance, with an almost unlimited
capacity for both mental and bodily labor. There is

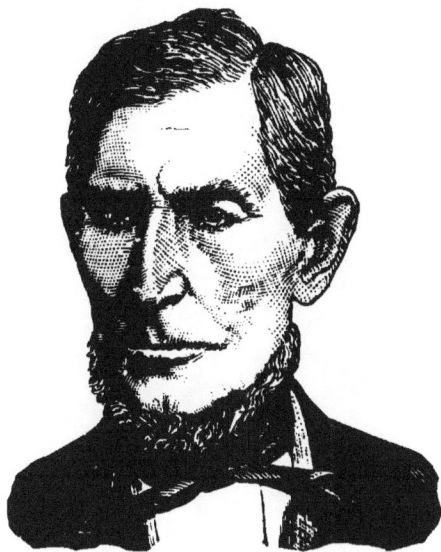

FIG. 8.—HON. JAS. D. WILLIAMS.

FIG. 9.—JAS. P. BECKWOURTH.

PHASES OF THE MOTIVE.

PLATE VI

never much superfluous flesh where the Motive Temperament is strongly predominant, and there is often more or less hollowness of cheeks, giving additional ruggedness to the features.

In women, to whom this Temperament is less proper than to man, and in whom it is far less common, the characteristics we have described are more or less modified, departing from the typical form in the direction of the rounder, more delicate, and softer contours, without losing the clear, definite, sharp lines which give the face and figure so striking an appearance. With the mental element nearly equal to the motive, and the vital not deficient, great elegance and a high order of beauty are often manifested, as in Mary Wortley Montagu (Fig. 10), Lucrezia Borgia, and others.

Children who inherit this Temperament (Fig. 12), and in whom active outdoor sports are permitted to give it facilities for development, are often very homely and awkward, but they improve as they reach maturity.

(2). The mental characteristics of the Motive Temperament are not less strongly marked than the physical. Its subjects are never mere " nobodies," but are sure to be known and noted for strong, positive traits of character. With an influential tempering with the brain element, they are everywhere the acknowledged leaders in the sphere of active life, where industry, energy, firmness, perseverance, indomitable courage, self-control, and executive ability are required and appreciated. They are men for the field rather than for the council chamber, and are often found at the head of armies and of great public works. They are observers rather than thinkers, and execute better than they plan. They are self-reliant, ambitious, proud, and sometimes arrogant, domineering, and cruel. They love power and conquest, and often pursue their ends with a reckless disregard for the physical welfare of both themselves and others. As speakers they use strong expressions, emphasize many words, and talk to the point, hitting the nail on the head with a heavy blow. In whatever way this temperamental condition may manifest itself, its manifestation will be forcible, open, and direct. Constancy in love and in friendship, and persistence in hostility and hatred may generally be counted upon in persons having this Temperament, especially when the dark or bilious element predominates.

With a marked deficiency in the mental element, there may be a very objectionable degree of coarseness and harshness of feelings, roughness and lack of susceptibility to all refining influences, indicated by a corresponding coarseness of fiber in the bodily organs, bushy hair and beard, and a harsh expression of countenance.

Great power and activity in some particular direction, rather than breadth and comprehensiveness, characterize those in whom this Temperament is indicated, and there is generally manifested a directness of purpose and a persistence in any determined course which nothing is permitted to change.

The Motive Temperament was common among the ancient Romans, and helped to make them masters of the world. In the Americans of the United States it is also very frequently met with, being with us next

FIG. 10.—MARY WORTLEY MONTAGU.

FIG. 11.—LITTLE CROW.

FIG. 12.—YOUTH.

PHASES OF THE MOTIVE.

PLATE VII.

in influence to our predominating mentality. It is strongly marked among the North American Indians (Fig. 11), and is not uncommon in Scotland, Ireland, Wales, and France. In America the States of Vermont, Maine, Kentucky, Tennessee, Missouri, and Arkansas are noted for its development. It prevails most in mountainous regions.

There is sometimes met with an abnormal development of the bony and muscular systems, in which both the vital and the mental elements are sacrificed to mere animal strength. This forms what the ancients called the Athletic Temperament. "It is marked by a head proportionally small, especially in the coronal region ; a thick neck ; broad shoulders ; expanded chest ; and strongly-marked muscles, the tendons of which are apparent through the skin. The Farnese Hercules furnishes a model of the physical attributes of this abnormal condition, in which brute strength usurps the energies necessary to the production of thought, and leaves its possessor decidedly deficient in all the higher mental and moral manifestations."

3. *Means of Culture.*—As the Motive Temperament depends upon those parts of the system, the hardest, most dense, and the slowest in undergoing the processes of growth and decay, it is less readily amenable to cultivation than the Vital and the Mental Temperaments ; nevertheless, it can be increased or diminished by persevering efforts in the proper direction in each case.

To promote the development, when desirable, of the locomotive system and its characteristic mental traits ;

(1). Choose for residence, when possible, a hilly or mountainous region, with a dry, stimulating atmosphere, and accustom yourself to labors or recreations calculated to make these advantages available and to call into constant action the whole muscular system, living and working, so far as possible, in the open air;

(2). Let your diet be composed in part of the muscular fiber of animals, with bread composed of unbolted wheat, and other substances containing considerable phosphate of lime and other bone-forming materials;

(3). Throw yourself heartily into the great currents of the world's progress, accepting and seeking opposition, discussion, and conflict of opinions. Seek positions of responsibility and those calling for the exercise of authority and the control of men, and involving the execution of important works. If war menace your country, and you can conscientiously take arms in its behalf, march to the front. Camplife and the clash of arms call out the elements of the Motive Temperament through the executive faculties of the brain, as well as by the direct culture of the bony and muscular systems.

4. *Counteractive Agencies.*—To counteract or modify any undue or hurtful development or to restrain the too violent manifestation of the harsher features of a predominant motive constitution, we must—

(1). Cultivate and encourage in every practicable way the antagonistic Vital organs, which predispose to geniality, love of ease, and a more cheerful, amiable disposition, as well as to versatility, vivacity, and sociability. The means for doing this are set forth under the head of Vital Temperament (Section 4, p. 78), which the reader may here consult;

(2). Develop, by exercise, the mental system, which has always a softening, elevating, and refining influence, favorable to the desired toning down of the somewhat hard and rough characteristics of a too domineering Motive Temperament. Poetry, *belles lettres*, music, and art are all influential agencies;

(3). Restrain the too violent action of the organs of Combativeness and Destructiveness, and oppose to Firmness and Self-esteem the modifying influences of Benevolence, Conscientiousness, and Approbativeness. The reasoning faculties, which are generally not so well developed, should be cultivated as naturally antagonistic to the predominant perceptives of this constitution.

II.—THE VITAL TEMPERAMENT (Fig. 13).

The physical basis of the Vital Temperament is found in the nutritive system, occupying the great cavities of the trunk and embracing the lymphatics, the blood-vessels, and the glands—in other words, the organs of absorption, circulation, and secretion. It includes the elements of both the Sanguine and the Lymphatic Temperaments of the old classification, and, in certain cases, a strong infusion of the bilious element, as we shall show further on.

1. *Causes.*—This is the Temperament of Childhood and its primary causes are to a large extent pre-natal. Among the most influential of those which promote its development after birth, as well as

(through the mother) during gestation, are the following:

(1). A climate calculated by its temperature and
atmospheric conditions to encourage and render
pleasant a large amount of outdoor exercise, and
neither so dry as to promote the density and hardness of muscle characteristic of the bilious constitution, nor so moist as to induce an abnormal development of lymph.

(2). Pleasurable employment or recreation, sufficient to keep all the bodily organs in tone and the
mind interested, without fatiguing or overtasking
either; with all the rest and sleep required for full
recuperation.

(3). Abundant, wholesome, nutritious, and easily-
digested food composed largely of farinaceous substances, to which is usually added, from the animal
kingdom, fat beef, mutton, and eggs, and from which
should be mainly excluded the more watery vegetables and all strong acids.

(4). Genial companionship; harmonious social relations; the free action of the affections, in all legitimate directions; the cultivation of the arts, and
especially music, and an easy, joyous, untrammeled
life generally, in which the violent passions—ambition, envy, jealousy, hate, etc.—have no part.

2. *Characteristics.*—(1). The Vital Temperament is
characterized, physically, by a stature above the
medium, and marked by a breadth and thickness of
body proportionally greater, and a size of limbs proportionally less than in the Motive Temperament.
The chest is full, the abdomen well developed, the

NORMAN McLEOD, D.D.

FIG. 13.—THE VITAL TEMPERAMENT.

PLATE VIII.

limbs plump, but tapering, and terminating in hands and feet relatively small. The neck is short and thick, the shoulders broad and well rounded, and the head and face, corresponding with the other parts of the system, incline to roundness. The expression of the countenance is generally lively, pleasing, frank, benevolent, and often mirthful. The pose of the body and its movements are natural, easy, graceful, and dignified. The pulse is quicker than in the Motive Temperament, and the organization throughout betokens vigor, warmth, and activity. The cheeks flush readily with exercise or emotion, and all the senses are active, acute, and refined.

The Vital Temperament, as we have defined it, includes the sanguine element of the constitution, which generally, in the Teutonic nations, gives its peculiar colors to the complexion, eyes, and hair; but cases occur in which all the essential physical characteristics of this Temperament are conjoined with the complexion which belongs to the bilious constitution. When we come to the Celtic nations this dark type is the prevailing one, as it is, of course, the universal one among the dark-skinned races, like the Indians and the Negroes.

Among the light-skinned and fair-haired branches of the Caucasian race these departures from the ordinary type of the Vital Temperament are doubtless often due to a strong bilious-motive tendency inherited from either the father or the mother, but overcome in every other direction by the still stronger Vital element, or by conditions peculiarly calculated to develop the nutritive system generally. Granting

4

this, however, does not change the aspects of the
case,·as it applies to the dark branches of the race,
among whom the Vital Temperament is as common
as with us—in fact, it is the prevailing one among the
Spaniards and their descendants, all swarthy, black-
haired people.

These considerations seem to require the recogni-
tion, as in the Motive Temperament, of two varieties
of this constitution, the light and the dark, or the
sanguine and the bilious. In the first the complexion is florid, the eyes blue, and the hair light ; in the
second the hair is black or dark brown, the eyes generally black or dark brown, but sometimes hazel oɪ
gray ; while the complexion may be swarthy, olive,
brown, copper-colored, yellow, or black. The dark
or bilious-vital variety is characterized physically
by more toughness and endurance and less activity
than the light or sanguine-vital.

An undue preponderance of the absorbent system,
conjoined with a sluggish action of the heart and
lungs, give rise to an abnormal deposit of watery
fluids under the skin, producing additional fullness,
and presenting softer and more rounded contours
than even those properly belonging to this constitution, but lacking their well-defined and graceful outlines.

This condition, when fully developed, constitutes
the Lymphatic Temperament of the old classification. A feeble leaden color of the skin, or lack of
expression in the countenance ; a flabbiness of the
flesh ; great sloth ; and general apathy, both of body
and mind, characterize this state of the system. Dr

Franklin, in his old age, showed something of this abnormal temperamental condition, as indicated in Fig. 15.

In a woman of this Temperament (which seems to be peculiarly the Temperament for women) the shoulders are softly rounded, but owe their breadth and thickness to the expanded chest, with which they are connected, rather than to the bones and muscles of the shoulders themselves; the bust is full and rounded; the waist proportional, but, as it were, somewhat encroached upon by the plumpness of the contiguous parts; the limbs tapering; the feet and hands small, but plump; the complexion (in the sanguine type) rosy; the eyes blue; and the hair flaxen, yellow, brown, or auburn. In the dark or Bilious variety, similar physical characteristics prevail, except that there is more density and hardness of fiber; less fineness and delicacy of skin and hair; an olive or brunette complexion; black or dark brown hair; and dark eyes. In both varieties the figure, as a whole, is full, soft, and voluptuous. Persons of this Temperament have greater vigor, but less toughness than those of the Motive Temperament. They love fresh air and exercise, and must be always doing something to work off the constantly accumulating stock of vitality; but they generally like play better than hard work.

(2). In correspondence with the vigor and activity with which all the bodily functions are performed, the mental processes are characterized by quickness, facility, and versatility, and the disposition by ardor, impulsiveness, and enthusiasm. Persons of this Temperament are distinguished by elasticity rather than firmness, and possess more diligence than persistence, and more brilliancy than depth. Ready perceptions, rapid deductions, active imagination, and vivacity of expression, enable them to make the impression of much more real talent and power than they actually possess. They are showy rather than solid; incapable of fixing the mind long upon one object, they are unfitted for the culture of the positive abstract sciences. They are subject to violent fits of passion, but are as easily calmed as excited; are generally lively, cheerful, amiable, genial, kind, good-natured, frank, and candid; always fond of good living, and more apt than others to fall into excesses in eating and drinking, and especially to become addicted to the intemperate use of stimulants. They find enjoyment in the mere sense of animal existence, and take for their motto, " Let us live while we live." As speakers and writers, they are ready, fluent, flowery, and impassioned. Their opinions are often adopted without much reflection, and are liable to be often changed. In friendship and in love they are ardent and sincere; but the volatility of their characters renders them sometimes inconstant and untrustworthy. They are impatient of restraint, and their strong social affections and fondness for good living are liable, unless restrained, to lead them into courses of frivolity and dissipation. With high moral principles to elevate them above such dangers, they generally lead happy and useful if not very noteworthy lives. Several brilliant writers and speakers have had this Temperament, with the mental system influential, but not dominant. Fig. 14 illustrates this statement,

FIG. 14.—MRS. C. B. PFEIFFER.

FIG. 15.—BENJAMIN FRANKLIN.

PHASES OF THE VITAL TEMPERAMENT.

PLATE IX.

and indicates the character of the talent associated with the predominance of the vital constitution, which—though perhaps incompatible with genius—often manifests a degree of practicable ability which passes with the public for more than genius, because not so far above the level of common thought and general experience.

It should be noted here, that where a dark complexion, black hair, and black or brown eyes are found associated with a strongly-developed vital system—that is, in the Bilious-Vital Temperament—there is always manifested a strength of passion, a depth of feeling, and a capacity for sustained effort and permanence of impression and affection—in a word, a force of character greater than in the *xanthous* class, while, on the other hand, there is less refinement, delicacy, vivacity, and amiability.

3. *Means of Culture.*—The agencies to be made use of to increase and develop the vital system, when deficient, will suggest themselves on recalling what has been said of the primary causes of the temperamental condition desired. We will, however, repeat:

(1). Where circumstances permit, choose for residence a mild, but not too hot and dry a climate, where abundant exercise in the open air will be practicable and pleasant, and adopt some occupation which will allow such exercise to be taken daily, if it be not found in the occupation itself, avoiding, by all means, sedentary employments and exclusion from the full enjoyment of the sunlight. Systematic gymnastic exercises, calculated to expand the chest and increase the power of the heart and lungs, should be taken when practicable. Rest and sleep must never be stinted, and the system never over-tasked.

(2). A nutritious diet, composed of easily digested articles of food, selected from both the animal and the vegetable kingdoms; from the former, beef and mutton, in good proportion (provided the digestive system will permit), fish and fresh eggs; and from the latter, farinaceous articles, such as Graham bread, oatmeal in various forms, rice, tapioca, cornmeal, etc., avoiding strong acids and watery vegetables. In all cases the healthful action of the digestive organs is all-important, as the best selection of food will be of no avail where the assimilation is imperfect.

(3). Cheerful companionship; pleasant surround-ings; freedom from care; the full legitimate satisfac-tion of the domestic and social affections; and in-tellectual activity, without hard study or continuous application.

4. *Counteractive Agencies.*—A condition of body and mind so conducive to enjoyment, as well as suc-cess in life, as the Vital Temperament has been shown to be, need seldom, it would seem, to be sub-jected to any measures calculated to counteract its tendencies or restrain its full activity; nevertheless, even the Vital constitution may be in excess, and, being so, lead to grave evils. It is as necessary, therefore, here, as in regard to the other Tempera-ments, to consider the means to lessen its relative power, or to modify its action. The most powerful counteractive agencies are:

(1). The increased activity (leading to increased development) of the muscular and nervous systems, through such exercises and culture as are best calculated to develop their strength and increase their relative influence in the constitution. Constant muscular exercise; a close application to business; a systematic study of some scientific subject; in short, full employment for both mind and body, will tend to increase both the muscular and the nervous or mental systems, and correspondingly depress the too active vital powers. Fat and carbonaceous foods, puddings, pastry, butter, sugar, cream, and milk should be avoided, and a less stimulating diet of cooling vegetables and acid fruits, with lean meats, be substituted.

(2). Where the predominant activity of the social affections, the love of good living and jovial companionship are likely to lead to excesses and dissipations hurtful alike to mind and body, every effort, in addition to the means suggested in the preceding paragraph, should be made to awaken and develop the moral sentiments, and especially those imparting a sense of right and wrong, self-respect and responsibility; thus may the impulsive, irrepressible activities of this Temperament be turned into channels of innocent recreation and honorable work, if not into those leading to great and heroic deeds, instead of finding their gratification in the paths of folly and vice.

The proneness of persons of this Temperament to become addicted to the excessive use of intoxicating drinks and to gluttonous habits, should be impressed

upon the minds of the young who are endowed with
its superabundant vitality, impulse, and passion, and
habits of strict control over appetite be early established.

III.—THE MENTAL TEMPERAMENT (Fig. 16).

Though the last of the three primary Temperaments to be described, this stands first in the order
of influence, the constitutional element on which it
depends being the leading one in the organization
of the civilized man, as it includes the brain, as well
as the sympathetic, sensory, and motor nerves associated with it in mental manifestation; and it has far
more influence upon the other temperamental conditions than they are able to exert upon it.

1. *Causes.*—The primary causes of the Mental
Temperament are the causes of human elevation, of
intellectual progress, of refinement, of literature and
art—in short, of civilization. Among barbarous
tribes it is seldom found, and among savages perhaps never. It is generally inherited from one or
both of the parents, but may be superinduced upon
a constitution in which it originally held a secondary
place, by means of a course of training directed to
that end.

(1). By studies and employments calling into full
and continuous activity the intellectual faculties, and
especially those most concerned in tracing the connection ·between cause and effect and in analytical
and synthetic processes.

(2). By association with cultivated .people, in the
midst of books, pictures, music, and other refining
influences.

CARDINAL MANNING.

FIG. 16.—THE MENTAL TEMPERAMENT.

PLATE X.

(3). By a diet and regimen of such a character as to foster brain rather than bone, muscle, or fat—eggs, fish, the flesh of poultry, nuts and cream for instance, as foods.

2. *Characteristics.*—(1). The Mental Temperament is characterized physically by a frame relatively slight, and a head relatively large; an oval face; a high, pale forehead, broadest at the top; delicately cut if not sharp features; an expressive countenance; a delicate, transparent skin; fine, soft hair, generally light in color and not abundant; brilliant, speaking eyes, generally gray or hazel, and quick in their movements; and a high-keyed, flexible voice. The figure is often elegant and graceful, but seldom striking or commanding. The muscles are small, but well formed, and adapted to rapid action, rather than to strength. Fineness and delicacy characterize the whole structure; but there is not necessarily any lack of real stamina, as the healthiness and longevity of persons of this constitution (when it be not subjected to great abuse) abundantly show. The brain is the great reservoir of power, but there must be a fountain of vitality behind it, from which it may draw. The Mental and Vital systems are closely correlated and act and re-act upon each other in the most harmonious manner, in a well-regulated life, but may be drawn into the direst antagonism by the abuse or abnormal action of either.

In women of this Temperament, though they are often very beautiful, there is a decided lack of the *embonpoint* which characterizes the Vital Temperament. The chest and bosom are only moderately

4*

developed and the pelvis is generally comparatively narrow, betokening a lesser degree of adaptation to the distinctive offices of the sex, than in the preceding Temperaments.

(2). Mentally this Temperament indicates activity of brain, acuteness of the senses, and intensity of emotion. The feelings are refined, the taste excellent, the conceptions vivid, the imagination lively and brilliant, and the moral sentiments generally active and influential. Persons of this Temperament generally manifest a decided taste for literature, and especially for poetry, love the fine arts and the beautiful in all its innumerable forms, and often display great talent as writers and artists, if not absolute genius—it being, in fact, the literary and artistic, and particularly the poetic Temperament. As the coronal organs of the brain are generally largely developed, and the basilar organs moderately so, good taste, delicacy of feelings, and refined manners render those in whom the Mental Temperament is influential, adverse to dissipation and degrading vices, and they seldom become criminals, drunkards, or debauchees; but when they do give themselves up to a career of crime, they become most dangerous enemies to society and are often able to evade justice for a long time. When their punishment comes, it is terrible, in proportion to their sensitiveness and capacity for suffering.

There is in this age, and especially in America, an excessive or morbid development of the nervous system which is most inimical to health, happiness, and longevity. It prevails particularly among women

FIG. 17.—MISS FRANCES E. WILLARD.

FIG. 18.—CHAS. H. PAYNE, D.D., L.L. D.

PHASES OF THE MENTAL TEMPERAMENT.

PLATE XII

(to whom even in its normal predominance it is less proper than the preceding), and answers to the Nervous Temperament of the old classification. It is characterized by the smallness and emaciation of the muscles, the quickness and intensity of the sensations, the suddenness and fickleness of the determinations, and a morbid impressibility. It is caused by sedentary habits; lack of bodily exercise; a premature and disproportionate development of the brain, through a false system of education; the immoderate use of tea and coffee; late hours; and other hurtful indulgencies.

3. *Means of Culture.*—Since the brain is the ruling element in the Mental Temperament, it is naturally mainly through that organ that it is to be effectively developed, though other means are available for auxiliary use in the work:

(1). Reading, systematic study, devotion to intellectual pursuits, habits of consecutive thinking, the study and practice of art or literature, cultivated society, and pleasant and tasteful—if possible, beautiful—surroundings are among the instrumentalities, acting directly through the mind, which may be made use of to promote the end in view.

(2). As an auxiliary physical influence, a diet calculated to nourish nerve and brain rather than bone and muscle—such articles of food as fish, eggs, the flesh of poultry and game, nuts, and milk are among the substances to be selected—should be perseveringly adhered to, not excluding, however, the variety essential to health.

4. *Counteractive Agencies.*—Where it is necessary

to correct a tendency to excessive mental action, liable to result in exhaustion and disease, the means to be resorted to are, in part—

(1). A partial or, temporarily, an entire withdrawal from active mental effort, giving the brain time to rest and recuperate.

(2). Recreation for mind and body in travel, in social enjoyments, and in various outdoor amusements.

(3). The sedulous cultivation of the vital or nutritive system, for the purpose of developing its various organs, and of giving them a greater relative influence in the constitution. To this end let the diet and regimen be such as are recommended for the purpose in Section II.

IV.—A Balance of Temperaments (Fig. 19).

There is an ideal condition to which the ancients gave the name of *Temperamentum temperatum*—the Temperate Temperament—in which all the constitutional elements—the Motive, the Vital and the Mental, or the Bilious, the Sanguine, the Lymphatic, and the Nervous—are perfectly in equilibrium. This is constitutional perfection. It has perhaps never yet been reached, but we occasionally meet persons in whom there is so close an approach to it that we are accustomed to speak of them as having a Balanced or Harmonious Temperament, it being difficult to determine which element is in predominance. Washington (Fig. 20), in his prime, seems to have presented a good example of this approximate balance of the

ROBERT COLLYER.

FIG. 19.—WELL-BALANCED TEMPERAMENT.

PLATE XII

temperamental elements. Later in life the lymphatic system appears to have assumed a larger degree of influence, indisposing him to all ambitious aspirations, as well as to all unnecessary exertion of body or mind.

With a balance of temperamental conditions, we find a well-developed, symmetrical body; shapely limbs; regular features; an evenly-formed cranium, with no sharp protuberances; a strong, regular pulse; a complexion often rather dark, but sometimes fair; brown hair, and gray, hazel, or brown eyes.

Mentally the same harmonious relations between the various faculties prevail. The vivacity, quickness, impulsiveness, and ardor of the Vital Temperament are modified by the cooler, slower, and more persistent Motive or Bilious element, and refined and elevated by the largely-developed mental constitution, while the intellectual force, taste, refinement, and delicacy of the Mental Temperament are imbued with warmth and vigor by the powerful Vital system, and made steadfast, enduring, and practical by the influential Motive development. Persons so constituted have a symmetrical, many-sided character, can do many things equally well, and are fitted to fill, with honor to themselves and usefulness to society, almost any position in life; and they will generally keep on the even tenor of their way, regardless of the trifling obstacles or the temporary attractions which turn less firmly established characters out of their proper course. The time may come in the great future, so pregnant with wonderful possibilities, when this harmonious development of person and character will be the prevailing one, and all lack of perfect balance in either body or mind be accounted abnormal.

V.—Compound Temperaments.

We have described in this chapter three Temperaments, which, as therein defined, present an exhaustive analysis of the human constitution, for, unless we admit the reality of the ideal condition just referred to as the Balanced Temperament, there must in each individual case be a predominance of one or the other of the three systems of organs on which the Temperaments are founded, and it is that predominance which determines the constitutional tendency, which is tempered or modified by the other elements in proportion to the development and activity of each. Practically, however, it is sometimes convenient to consider the Temperaments as compounded, and to give definite names to the conditions recognized to exist in consequence of certain combinations. For instance, two of the constitutional elements may be strongly developed, and nearly, but not quite, equal in their influence, while the third is comparatively weak. The two strong elements then determine the compound, which we name by placing first the designation of the dominant one followed by that of the next in power. In this way we may, with some practical advantage, perhaps, form six Compound Temperaments, as follows:

 1. The Motive-Vital Temperament;
 2. The Motive-Mental Temperament;
 3. The Vital-Motive Temperament;
 4. The Vital-Mental Temperament;

FIG. 20.—GEORGE WASHINGTON.

FIG. 21.—JENNY LIND.

PHASES OF WELL-BALANCED TEMPERAMENT.

PLATE XIII.

5. The Mental-Motive Temperament; and

6. The Mental-Vital Temperament.

The names of these Compound .Temperaments sufficiently indicate their character. The Motive-Vital and the Vital-Motive differ but little, comparatively—the name placed first, as we have said, in either case, indicating the stronger influence; and the same remark applies to the Motive-Mental and the Mental-Motive, and to the Vital-Mental and to the Mental-Vital.

1. *The Motive-Vital Temperament* (Fig. 22).—For mere animal power, this is the combination that would be desired above all others. Bone and muscle fully developed; strongly-hinged joints; ligaments of iron and tendons of steel; broad shoulders; full chest; abundant vitality; firmness, toughness, steadiness, and activity all combined. There may be awkwardness, but there must be immense capacity for hard work, great endurance, and the necessary perseverance to carry out any movement or enterprise once commenced.

This combination is not an intellectual one; but while there will be little taste for literature or art, and no love of study, or even of reading, there may be much practical business talent, clear perceptions, and a cool, sound judgment, in ordinary every-day affairs. Many excellent people have this Temperament, as well as some of the most depraved of criminals. Strong passions, envy, hate, revenge, and cruelty characterize it in its worst aspects, when unrestrained by the moral faculties and unrefined by an influential development of the mental system.

Pugilists, sailors, soldiers, farmers, and others whose pursuits necessitate much muscular exercise in the open air, often have the Motive-Vital Temperament.

2. *The Motive-Mental Temperament* (Fig. 23).— Supposing the motive system still dominant, we now substitute for the Vital or nutritive element, as next in order of influence, the Mental constitution, the former being subordinate to both, though not necessarily weak. This combination gives us intellectual power, combined with bodily strength, toughness, and endurance. The figure is slenderer than in the Motive-Vital Temperament, but tough, wiry, and active. The features are prominent, often homely, but never mean or vulgar-looking, having the stamp of intelligence, if not refinement, upon them. The hair and complexion are generally rather dark, and the eyes brown or gray. The pose of the body is firm, the walk rapid and energetic, and the elocution clear, distinct, and forcible.

Persons of this temperamental combination are clear-headed, vigorous thinkers, and bold, energetic, and persevering in action. Their strong passions are not always well controlled, but the restraining influences of the æsthetic faculties and moral sentiments are stronger than in the Motive-Vital organization. Solid learning, grave and earnest feelings, practical talent, ambition, desire, and ability to lead in great undertakings, and to rise to eminence in the spheres of active life and scientific investigation, characterize their mental constitution, which is that of some of the greatest men that the world has ever produced—warriors, explorers, engineers, navigators,

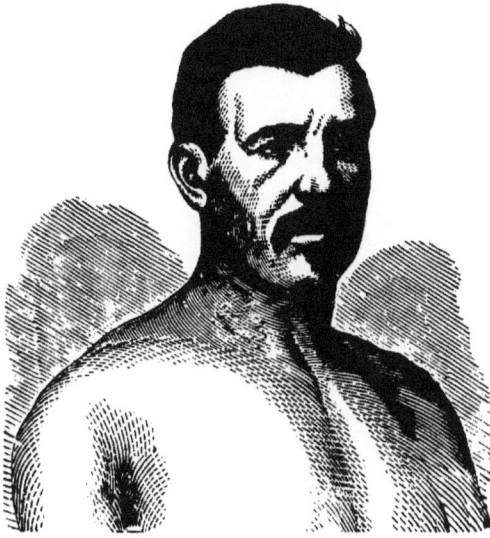

FIG. 22.—MOTIVE-VITAL. JOHN C. HEENAN.

FIG. 23.— MOTIVE-MENTAL. JOHN ORTON.

PLATE XIV.

and men of action generally, while being men of thought at the same time—capable alike of planning and of executing great enterprises. It is a very common one among Americans, especially those whose pursuits are of an active character, and who have not been subjected to premature and excessive mental culture.

3. *The Vital-Motive Temperament* (Fig. 24). — A large, broadly-developed body; broad shoulders; thick neck; muscular and strong-jointed, but rounded limbs, combined with prominent features; a somewhat harsh expression, coarse hair, ruddy complexion (if of the Caucasian race), and strong and rapid, but seldom graceful movements, characterize this combination. There will be great capacity for hard work, a strong love for outdoor muscular exercise, and an invincible repugnance to confinement and restraint. The Vital element predominating, there may be considerable vivacity and impulsiveness, much restrained, however, by the cooler and more equable tendencies imparted by the Motive element. The talent displayed by persons of this Temperament will never be showy or brilliant, but of a practical character, and manifested in business or work, rather than in literary expression. Good common sense and ability to manage well, rather than a display of superficial accomplishments, mark the mental character. Morally, persons of this constitutional combination have generally strong passions and active appetites to contend against, and are liable to be led into dissipation, intemperance, and crime, through their strong animality, unless the moral sentiments

be well developed, and the restraining influences of cultivated society and religious training shall hold the lower nature in check. Savages, and unlettered men in civilized society, frequently possess this temperamental condition, but it is also found in the higher social spheres.

4. *The Vital-Mental Temperament* (Fig. 25).—In this combination we find a plump, well-rounded figure; a full and rather large face ; handsome features, not very prominent, but well-defined and often regular; complexion fair and rosy; eyes blue; hair yellow, light brown, or auburn ; expression lively, ardent, and amiable. It sometimes exists in men, but oftener in women, to whom it imparts many lovable traits— peculiarly desirable in the fair sex—warm affections, kindness, amiability, and liveliness, combined with personal beauty and grace. It is a pleasure-loving Temperament, however, and its vigorous appetites and active passions often require strong restraining agencies to keep them under proper control. Men of this constitution are suited to active outdoor employments, and, if well educated, make good public speakers, though they will not be noted for solid acquirements, thorough investigation, or deep thought; being rather brilliant and showy than sound and original. In their speaking and writing they are generally fluent, and often florid and somewhat verbose. They are rapid, but graceful in their motions, and gesticulate much in speaking.

5. *The Mental-Motive Temperament* (Fig. 26).— Persons of this Temperament are characterized by a tall and rather spare figure, somewhat inclined to an-

FIG. 24.—VITAL-MOTIVE. DAVID DAVIS.

FIG. 25.—VITAL-MENTAL. QUEEN EMMA.

COMPOUND TEMPERAMENTS.

PLATE XV.

gularity, but often dignified and striking in appearance, and firm and upright in pose. The features are generally rather prominent, but clearly cut and refined ; the expression serious and grave; the eyes gray, hazel, or brown ; the hair generally light brown ; the complexion often brilliant (brown on the cheeks, but paler on the forehead); the voice clear, high-keyed, and flexible ; and the walk firm and direct.

With a fair development of the Vital system, this temperamental combination gives an assurance of intellectual power, combined with executive ability, fitting its possessor for the achievement of notable success, either in literature, the arts and sciences, or in the more active pursuits of life ; though there is sometimes a lack of balance in the mental organization, which leads to fruitless efforts and a sad waste of talent and energy. The reflective faculties generally predominate over the perceptives, giving excellent planning ability, discrimination, sound judgment, and forecaste. Those who possess it manifest great fondness for literature of the graver and more solid kind, a love of scientific studies and pursuits, and generally superior talents as thinkers, writers, and workers in their chosen spheres. It is the organization best adapted to authorship, and counts among its possessors many of the most eminent literary men of all ages and nations. The moral tone is generally high, the animal propensities being relatively weak, and in subjection to the intellect and the higher sentiments.

6. *The Mental-Vital Temperament* (Fig. 27).—This organization combines so many desirable qualities of body and mind that one is inclined to envy its fortunate

possessors; but the world does not find among them.
its greatest leaders and benefactors. They are more
exalted, amiable, and brilliant than solid, strong, firm,
and persistent. In person, they are rather below the
average in stature; moderately full in form and face;
and with well-proportioned, tapering limbs. The
features are not prominent, but well-defined, and
often very regular and handsome. The expression
is full of intelligence, sweetness, and sympathy. The
complexion is fair, the hair brown or auburn, and the
eyes gray or blue. An active brain, versatility of talent, literary and artistic tastes, strong domestic and
social feelings, exalted moral and religious sentiments,
and great amiability, benevolence, tenderness, and
purity of character generally characterize the mental
manifestations of this Temperament; but it lacks
the force, directness, and energy of the mental-motive
organization. It is not confined to the fair sex, but
is more common among women than among men.
In either sex it generally gives a clear, active, versatile mind; much good nature; warm affections,
and great moral worth, together with a full share of
vital stamina and beauty of person. Orators, poets,
novelists, and artists, though not the greatest of
either, have had this combination of temperamental
conditions.

V.

TEMPERAMENT AND CONFIGURATION.

IN our brief synoptical description of the various Temperaments in previous chapters, we have spoken in a general way of the configuration of the body and the features of the face peculiar to each ; but it will be profitable, as greatly aiding in the practical application of the knowledge we have endeavored to impart, to enter somewhat more into detail upon several of the more important points involved in the delineation of Temperaments, and among the rest the relations existing between constitutional qualities and external forms.

It may be unnecessary, but, at worst, it will do no harm, to again caution the reader against falling into the error of assuming that any general rule that we, or any one, can give, or any detailed description, will apply in every particular to all cases which may come under observation. The numerous combinations of which the primary elements of Temperament are susceptible, and the difficulty of determining accurately the relative influence of each in the organization, should make even the experienced student of physiology and of mental science exceedingly careful in his comparison of the different characteristics, and put him on his guard against deciding upon a Temperament by any one indication or class of indications alone. The general configuration of the body may seem to indicate one Temperament, while the features or the complexion may as clearly point to another; the eyes and the hair may plainly contradict each other; and even, as is not infrequently the case, the hair of the head and the beard may symbolize opposite mental and temperamental traits. These are departures from the symmetry and homogeneousness which should, theoretically, characterize an organism, and are due to inharmonious crosses and other disturbing causes, generally pre-natal in their action. A full knowledge of all the circumstances, including both hereditary transmission and external influences, acting after birth, not always readily attainable, would, no doubt, explain all seeming inconsistencies. In the meantime, it is not wise to lose faith in general laws because we can not account for all observed apparent exceptions.

I.—CONFIGURATION IN THE MOTIVE TEMPERAMENT (Figs. 28 to 31).

As the Motive Temperament depends upon the predominance of the locomotive apparatus, consisting of the bones, muscles, and ligaments which form the framework of the body, we may naturally expect here the most definite, strongly expressed, and prominent contours, and such, in fact, we find. The bones are large, long rather than broad, and much bulged at the joints, forming a tall and striking rather than an elegant figure, characterized by angularity rather than roundness, and giving, with the help of the strong, wiry muscles, an impression of strength rather

FIG. 26.—MENTAL-MOTIVE. ELIHU BURRITT.

FIG. 27.—MENTAL-VITAL. DUTCHESS MARIE OF SAXONY.

COMPOUND TEMPERAMENTS.

PLATE XVI.

than of grace or refined beauty. The face, from which, mainly, we must draw our illustrations, is, in the full front view, oblong, as in Fig. 30, approaching, in some cases, as in Fig. 29, to the rectilinear, the latter being an exclusively masculine type. The features are prominent, presenting in profile strong angularities and abrupt curves, as shown in the outline (Fig. 28) and in the portrait. In the latter, however, in consequence of the strength and predominance of the mental element, which, in proportion to its influence in the constitution, modifies the frontal outlines by giving more expansion to the forehead, there is less harshness in the contours than in the Motive physiognomy not thus softened. A more influential admixture of the Vital element imparts a greater relative breadth to the lower part of the face, and a more rounded outline, in which is indicated immense physical power, toughness, and endurance, with a corresponding force of character and intellectual efficiency.

In strict harmony with the head, face, and body, the hands (Fig. 31) of persons in whom the Motive Temperament is fully developed, are long and bony, with prominent joints and strong ligaments—hands of action and power, whose grasp is firm and assuring, and whose blows are hard and unerring, careless alike of hurting and of being hurt. The clasp of such a hand can generally be trusted in pledge of friendship or love. Beware of it if lifted against you in enmity. The feet are of similar structure.

II.— CONFIGURATION IN THE VITAL TEMPERA-
MENT (Figs. 32 to 35).

The predominance of the nutritive system, occupying the great cavities of the trunk, which
furnishes the physical basis of the Vital Temperament, tends to give breadth and thickness to the
body as a whole, and to all its individual members.
Its most striking characteristic, therefore, is plumpness or rotundity. The figure, though its stature
may be above the medium, does not appear tall, but
leaves the impression of fullness and symmetry.
Looking at the head and face from the front we get
an outline closely approaching the circular, as in Fig.
32. The portraits of distinguished men furnish no
examples belonging strictly to this class, though
many noted persons have presented contours more
or less closely approaching the typical form; the face
proper having the necessary roundness, but the elevation of the forehead, consequent upon prominent
mentality, modifying very strikingly the outlines of
the whole facial expanse, as seen in Fig. 31. Napoleon
and Peter the Great were notable examples of this
modification of the round form of face, their Temperament being Mental-Vital. Sometimes the lower
nature gets the mastery, or a diseased condition of
the lymphatic system gives a flabby fullness to the
lower part of the face.

A side view of the head and face gives the characteristic curves of this temperamental condition as
plainly as the front, the features all being more or
less gracefully rounded, as shown in Fig. 35.

FIG. 28.—PROFILE.

FIG. 29.—J. D. B. DE BOW.

FIG. 30.—WM. REEVES, D.D.

FIG. 31.—HAND.

CONFIGURATION OF THE MOTIVE.

PLATE XVII.

In the profile of Franklin, as he appeared in old age (Fig. 15), we have an illustration of both the modifications referred to in the preceding paragraph —the predominating intellectuality in the frontal region of the cranium, and an abnormal lymphatic condition of the physical system in the lower part of the face.

The hand (Fig. 34) in this Temperament is broad and full rather than long. The palm is round and soft ; and the fingers plump and tapering ; the veins, arteries, and tendons invisible ; and the whole organ symmetrical, and, though rather heavy, not large in proportion to the other parts of the body. Its grasp is soft, warm, and hearty, but not always so trustworthy in time of trial as that of the more homely long hand. It is the hand of vivacity and versatility, and loves its ease and cherishes its softness and flexibility too much to be fond of rude labors or of dealing deadly blows. It prefers the pen to the sword, and may write with fervor and brilliancy, but hardly with great strength of style or originality of thought.

III.—CONFIGURATION IN THE MENTAL TEMPERAMENT (Figs. 36 to 39).

In this Temperament, the brain and nervous system being predominant, the bones and muscles are comparatively thin, and the vital organs less voluminous than in either of the other Temperaments. The frame is therefore slight, and the stature generally below the medium, and calculated to exhibit elegance and grace rather than dignity and force.

5

The chief seat and center of this constitution being within the dome of the cranium, the head is relatively large, and the expansion of the superior parts of the face, including the forehead, give a pyriform or pear-shaped outline, as so strikingly shown in the accompanying portraits (Figs. 36 and 37). This is the literary, artistic, and particularly the poetic form of face, as illustrated in Shakespeare, Dante, Tennyson, Keats, Rubens, Flaxman, and many others.

In profile, the pyriform face presents lines less angular than those of the oblong or Motive form, and less rounded than those of the circular or Vital form, but finer and more delicate than either. Such faces are not necessarily beautiful, in the ordinary conception of that term, but there is always an undefinable air of refinement and spirituality about them not observed in any other form.

Where such outlines as we have here described and illustrated are observed in the faces of children (which should have the round or Vital configuration) they indicate a strong inherited predisposition to the Mental Temperament, likely, unless counteracted by the judicious cultivation of the vital and motive elements of the constitution (the mental meanwhile being held in as passive a condition as possible), to result in an intellectual precociousness hurtful in the extreme to mind and body alike and often fatal to the latter.

The small bones, thin muscles, and slight articulations characteristic of the Mental Temperament, are particularly noticeable in the hand (Fig. 39), which is slender and often graceful, expressive of delicacy

FIG. 32.—CATHARINE ALEXIEONA.

FIG. 33.—ABRAHAM DE SOLA.

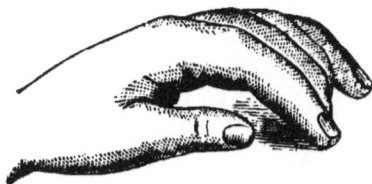

FIG. 34.—HAND.

FIG. 35.—PROFILE.

CONFIGURATION OF THE VITAL TEMPERAMENT.

PLATE XVIII.

and refinement. It is not well adapted to heavy labor, and shrinks, as a matter of taste, from contact with the sword-hilt, though a high moral sentiment of patriotism or of religion may overcome the peaceful instinct and give it the subtle, but strong, stimulus of brain-power to make its blows like strokes of lightning. It is naturally artistic, poetic, and exclusive, having a friendly grasp for a *few* and a tender, loving clasp for *one*.

SIR JOHN LUBBOCK.—MENTAL-MOTIVE.

VI.

TEMPERAMENT AND COLOR.

THE different shades of the complexion and the color of the eyes, hair, and beard, furnish important indications of temperamental conditions, and may, with advantage to the reader, be here more fully elucidated; though the subject is one which has been too little investigated to afford an extensive array of facts or to warrant many positive deductions. To go into any elaborate discussion of the philosophy of color, moreover, were that not otherwise inexpedient, would lead us too far away from the practical ends we have in view and needlessly complicate our subject. We shall, therefore, confine our preliminary enunciation to the single generally accepted physiological and physiognomical principle, that dark colors, whether found in the skin, the eyes, or the hair, indicate power, and light colors delicacy, the general law being subject to the modifications of race, climate, and other circumstances. Our remarks in this chapter will refer to the Caucasian race, leaving the ethnological peculiarities of Temperament to be discussed in another chapter.

I.—THE MELANIC ELEMENT IN TEMPERAMENT (Figs. 40 to 42).

It is the bilious element in the constitution that imparts the dark hues, while the sanguine gives us

FIG. 36.—RACHEL.

FIG. 37.—KEATS.

FIG. 38.—PROFILE.

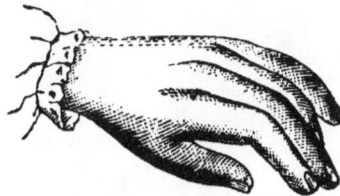

FIG. 39.—HAND.

CONFIGURATION OF THE MENTAL TEMPERAMENT.

PLATE XIX.

the red and blue, and the nervous the white. Where the liver and its closely associated organs predominate in influence, we find dark complexions, or at least dark hair and eyes; the ascendency of the arterial system and the lungs manifests itself in a florid skin and blue eyes; and dominant mentality is generally associated with gray eyes and a complexion intermediate between the two others, the colors exhibited being due to the combination, in varying proportions, of the dark and the light elements.

The dark bilious or *melanic* element, though in the light-skinned branches of the Caucasian race more generally associated with the Motive Temperament, is by no means confined to it, being found in numerous instances in connection with a large and influential development of the vital system, as in Webster and Napoleon. In both these celebrated men there was a marked predominance of the nutritive over the osseous and muscular systems, and yet both had dark eyes and hair and a dark complexion—in the former, swarthy; in the latter, olive or tawny. The domination of the brain in both these cases does not affect the principle, since the coloring matters come alone from the organs concerned in the functions of mere animal life, the nervous system (including the brain), as we have said, expressing itself in palor or whiteness.

Turning our attention to the Celtic or darker branch of the Caucasian race, we find the *melanic* element very generally associated with both the Motive and Vital Temperaments, and giving, in combination, a darker hue to the Mental. Especially is this the case with the Spanish peoples in Europe and America, who are almost universally dark-complex-ioned, with black hair and eyes.

On the other hand, no close observer of personal peculiarities, whether engaged in the study of the Temperaments or not, can have failed to note cases in which the strong, bony, angular frame, prominent features, and firm, decided movements, characteristic of the Motive Temperament, are conjoined with a florid complexion, light hair (especially red or auburn), and blue eyes. It is the sanguine element of the Vital Temperament manifesting itself in a single characteristic or group of characteristics, while in en-tire subordination elsewhere ; and the same remark will apply to those not infrequent instances in which the beard is light, while the hair is dark; or where blue eyes are seen in a brunette ; or red or yellow hair accompanies black or brown eyes. These are all cases in which the action of a general law is modified by the intervention of some special cause, such as the crossing of different families or races, pre-natal im-pressions, etc.

In regard to red hair, observation has convinced us that it is closely related, both physiologically and as a sign of Temperament and character, to black hair. In the crosses of the Negro with the Caucasian, black hair is the most persistent sign of the dark blood, holding its place after all trace of the African taint has disappeared from the complexion, and never furnishing examples of even the darkest brown, much less of yellow, but even in mulattoes (half-bloods) red hair or wool not very infrequently appears. Of this we have observed several instances in Charleston, S. C., and elsewhere.

Returning now to the consideration of the *melanic* element in Temperament, we observe that in the white races it indicates the bilious constitution, and manifests itself in dark (often black) hair and eyes, and a brown, tawny, or swarthy complexion, and that the Motive Temperament has, very generally among us, this feature, as it has others, in common with the Bilious.

In the *melanic* or dark variety of the Motive Temperament (which we denominate the Bilious-Motive) the features are harsher and more sharply outlined than in the light or *xanthous* type, so that, in general, the complexion and color of the hair and eyes can be pretty accurately determined by an examination of a correct uncolored portrait, especially in profile.

Fig. 40 is a striking, but by no means an attractive portrait, which may be referred to in illustration of the statement just made. We never saw the original. All that we know of him, beyond what the picture tells us, is that he was a ruthless desperado, and the leader of a band of robbers, who was finally captured and suffered "the extreme penalty of the law." We are told nothing of his Temperament, or of the color of his hair and eyes, or the tint of his complexion. There was little need to tell us anything on these points. None but black or dark brown eyes could, without a palpable incongruity, have looked out beneath those shaggy eyebrows, and no other color than black would have suited that coarse, bushy hair and beard, and those strong, not ill-formed, yet unlovely features, could have fitly worn no hue but a swarthy one. The profile of the Bedouin (Fig. 41) indicates the same constitutional condition and similar *melanic* hues; and a list of the world's great warriors, and vanquishers of obstacles generally, in all the spheres of active life—the exponents of *power*, of mind and body—from Cæsar to Napoleon, would embrace few names of men who have not been *tempered* by a large admixture of this element, dominated over invariably by a well-developed brain.

The dark-haired, swarthy, bilious man may be a beneficent power commissioned for the elevation and liberation of his fellow-men, but often he wields his tremendous physical and mental forces rather to satisfy his own selfish ends and minister to his ambition and love of power. He is never a nonentity, or a passive instrument in the hands of others. He always asserts his individuality, and claims leadership wherever hardships and dangers are to be encountered, and power or glory to be won.

The harsher physiognomical traits of the dark bilious, or melano-motive, type are often greatly softened in woman, and when modified by predominating intellectuality (constituting the Mental-Motive Temperament) it furnishes numerous examples of the highest order of female beauty, the mental element giving delicacy and refinement to the sharp, clear lines proper to the Motive Temperament, as seen in Fig. 36. The following brief, but graphic description of the great queen of tragedy as she appeared on the stage in her best days. will help the reader to a

FIG. 40.—TIBURCIO VASQUEZ.

FIG. 41.—A BEDOUIN ARAB.

TEMPERAMENT AND COLOR.

PLATE XX.

clearer idea of the *melanic* element in woman when associated with the Mental Temperament, the motive constitution being next in the order of potency:

"Pale, with jet-black hair; a small, regular nose; a mouth mobile enough, but rather sweet in its expression and tender in its lines for the heroine of tragedy; and a large forehead quite protruding itself over the straight, black brows that shadow her wondrous eyes, she is the very embodiment of feminine intellect. Her figure is slight, and her mental entirely dominates her vital system; but her limbs, with all their delicacy, have a firm look, and she is rather lithe than fragile. The fall of her drapery would make any sculptor despair, did he not see that itself is but the reproduction in tissue of lines into which the Grecian sculptors wrought their marble."

The dark element in human Temperament seems for a long time to have been on the increase. At the time of the Roman invasion of those countries, the inhabitants of Great Britain and France, as well as of Germany—Celts and Saxons alike—were blue-eyed and had red, yellow, or flaxen hair. No one seems to have taken note of the change while it was going on, but now the true Celt, whether French, Irish, or Highland Scotch, is very generally dark-haired, and the same change is evidently taking place in the Gothic races, and particularly in the Anglo-Saxon branch. Close observers are beginning to note this in Europe. Here, in America, the change is still more obvious and rapid. As a nation, we Americans of the United States are gradually becoming *melanic*. Cities seem to favor this temperamental condition,

5*

the proportion of dark-haired people being much greater there than in the country.

In some cases the indications of the blonde type linger in the beard for a generation or two after they have disappeared from the hair of the head ; so that many of the men of the present day have dark hair and yellow or sandy beards.

The color of the eyes and the tint of the complexion do not always follow the rule of the hair, but dark eyes and brown or swarthy cheeks are evidently increasing.

We might speculate here on the causes of the temperamental changes going on in the Caucasian races, and the probable results, but we prefer to leave such speculations to others, or for a more appropriate occasion, simply hinting that there is a constant tendency observable in living things—plants, animals, and men, alike—to adapt themselves, so far as the distinctions of race and species will permit, to all changes of external conditions, such as climate, food, and modes of life, and that these are by no means exactly the same now that they were in the time of Julius Cæsar, even in the countries overrun by the Romans, much less in this New World, which the ancient conquerors of the Old knew not.

II.—THE BLONDE ELEMENT IN TEMPERAMENT (Fig. 43).

Fair hair, blue eyes, and a light or florid complexion are associated with the sanguine element of the constitution, and generally, among us, indicate the Vital Temperament, or at least a very influential development of the nutritive system, and especially of the

FIG. 42.—THE BRUNETTE.

FIG. 43.—THE BLONDE.

TEMPERAMENT AND COLOR.

PLATE XXI.

organs of respiration and arterial circulation. In a majority of cases, they are found associated with full, finely-developed figures; faces inclining to roundness; full lips; wide nostrils; and a cheerful expression of countenance.

There are, however, as we have noted in the preceding section, cases in which these sanguine characteristics are found in connection with the more angular outlines of body and prominent features, indicative of the Motive Temperament. Many distinguished historical personages, and among them Gustavus Adolphus of Sweden, and the great epic poet of Italy, Tasso, were of this Sanguine-Motive type. The latter has the features of the Bilious-Motive class in perfection, but there was in his character much of the delicacy of the blonde, combined with the strength, persistence, and energy of the dark type. The predominance of the mental element of course greatly modified the action of both the others.

The Sanguine-Motive type is the common one among the Scandinavian peoples, and also among the Highland Scotch of the higher classes, who are doubtless of Norse origin.

In estimating the influence of Temperament on character, as well as in observing it as a sign of character, we must bear in mind the fact that the dark complexion is imparted by the bilious element, and the florid by the sanguine, while the mental or nervous (the brain imparting no color—or more accurately, combining all colors) gives whiteness.

III.—COMBINATIONS OF COLOR AND TEMPERA-
MENT.

A brilliant skin with a peachy bloom on the cheeks, sometimes showing a slightly sallow tinge, indicates a Mental-Motive Temperament of the bilious or dark type. The eyes in such cases may be either brown or gray. The hair is generally dark (often black) and fine, and the features clearly cut, but refined and delicate. The Motive-Mental Temperament presents similar forms and coloring, except that the hues are a little darker and the outlines harsher and more prominent.

The Mental-Vital Temperament presents the true pink and white skin, the red of the sanguine element taking the place of the black and yellow of the bilious constitution. The eyes are blue or light gray and the hair light and fine. Dante's Beatrice, if the existing portraits of her are correct, illustrated this combination. A larger infusion of the sanguine-vital element gives more red in the complexion and a deeper blue to the eyes. The hair is often red or auburn, and there is an expression of warmth and liveliness about the countenance which betokens rapidity of action and quickness of temper.

In the Vital-Motive Temperament we have the red of the sanguine element combined with a smaller proportion of the black or yellow of the bilious secretions, giving often a rich brown complexion, with brown or hazel eyes and brown hair. Where the Motive apparatus predominates, so as to give us the Motive-Sanguine Temperamental combination, there appears less red in the complexion, and the hair and eyes are generally darker, except in the *xanthous* or red-haired type.

A pale, dull, leaden hue in the complexion, dull, expressionless eyes, and faded-looking hair indicate that abnormal or sickly condition described by the pathologists as the Lymphatic Temperament.

Of the three organs to which we look for the indications of Temperamental conditions to be found in color, the skin furnishes the most trustworthy index, though even that is liable to mislead, where the health is not good. Actual disease must, of course, always be taken into account, where it exists. Color in the hair and eyes, more frequently than in the skin, varies from the hue which the other constitutional signs would seem to call for. As a general rule, however, there will be found little incongruity which can not be readily explained.

In our chapter on "Temperament in Races and Nations," it will be seen how the general principles enunciated and illustrated in the foregoing pages apply to the red, brown, yellow, and black races.

VII.

THE function of nutrition being the most important of the physical operations during the first years of life, young children generally (as they should in all cases) have the Vital Temperament; but there is inherent in each, inherited from its parents, a tendency to the development of a permanent temperamental condition, which may also be Vital, or it may be Motive or Mental. When once established, this Temperament inclines naturally to perpetuate and increase itself, since it gives rise to habits that exercise the organs on which it depends. A change of Temperament, then, implies strong counteracting influences brought to bear upon the constitution; and as such strong influences are, in a majority of cases, lacking, the inherited tendency is generally followed, and a Temperament once established is maintained through life. This, however, is far from being universally the case. The inherent predisposition is sometimes entirely overcome and the constitution radically changed. The means by which this change may be effected are both physical and mental, and have already, in treating of the causes of the Temperaments, been briefly stated. All that will be necessary here will be to speak of some of them a little more in detail, and with more direct reference to certain specified cases.

FIG. 44.—INFANCY.

FIG. 45 —CHILDHOOD.

FIG. 46.— GRACE GREENWOOD.

FIG. 47.—GRACE GREENWOOD.

CHANGES OF TEMPERAMENT.

PLATE XXII.

I.—CHANGES THROUGH NATURAL GROWTH.

In childhood there should be a relatively stronger development of the vital system than is exhibited in Fig. 45, which represents, perhaps too correctly, however, the average "smart" American boy of the period. Good, wholesome, nutritious food, pleasant surroundings, judicious training, and plenty of outdoor sports should keep the face round and full (as in Fig. 44), and the cheeks ruddy till childhood begins to merge in youth. Then suddenly there comes a change! The bones seem to expand preternaturally, the joints enlarge, the limbs outgrow their clothing, and even disturb the balance between themselves and the trunk. The graceful boy becomes an awkward youth. The Motive or bony and muscular element of the constitution now assumes predominance. If the Motive Temperament be the inherited one, it is at this period expressed in exaggerated forms, the youth being very tall, raw-boned, and angular; but in all cases of natural, healthy growth there is more or less of this sudden and powerful Motive influence.

When the period of rapid growth is over, unless some other powerful influence has been brought to bear to counteract it, the inherited tendency assumes its sway, and the Temperament becomes comparatively a fixed and permanent condition.

At the age of from forty to forty-five there manifests itself in some constitutions, showing previously decided Mental or Motive tendencies, a strong influx of the nutritive element, changing the sharp or angular outlines into the more rounded contours of the Vital Temperament. Something of this kind is illustrated by Figs. 46 and 47. This change takes place in both sexes, but oftener in women than in men.

Finally, in the old age of persons who have previously shown an influential development of the sanguine element of the Vital Temperament, there frequently occurs, as in the case of Dr. Franklin (Fig. 15), an access of the Lymphatic constitution, giving a flabby appearance to the lower parts of the face, and an unnatural softness and shapelessness to the features. This we do not consider a natural healthy condition, whether coming on in old age or earlier in life, though in the former case there may be simply a failure in the circulatory system to fully perform its functions.

II.—CHANGES FROM EXTERNAL INFLUENCES.

Altitude, heat and cold, moisture and dryness, all have an influence in forming, sustaining, or changing the Temperament and configuration of individuals, families, and races. " The inhabitants of the regions of gusty winds," Wilkinson says, " have weather-beaten faces, and lines as of the tempests blown howling into their skins. Mountain races have stony or granitic features, as of rocks abandoned to the barren air. The people of moist and marshy places look watery and lymphatic. Those where extremes of temperature prevail for long periods are leathern and shriveled, as though their skins had given up the contest and died upon their faces."

Persons removing from a cold to a warm country are subject to an access of the bilious element, often so great as to entirely overcome a previously sanguine predominance. On the other hand, removal from a warm to a colder climate stimulates the respiratory and arterial systems, and promotes a change in the opposite direction. These changes, perpetuated and increased from generation to generation, finally produce distinct Northern and Southern types. It is in temperate climates that we find the highest order of physical development and the closest approach to a balance of temperamental elements.*

A moist atmosphere, when not excessively humid and not malarious, promotes the Vital Temperament, the influence of the Motive element being lessened and the Mental becoming less active, from the lack of stimulus. Low, marshy regions, like Holland, induce, through moisture and malaria, that abnormal temperamental condition known as the lymphatic constitution. Persons removing from a region having a moist atmosphere, to one where dry winds pre-

---

* According to our own observations, which have extended from New Hampshire and Vermont on the north to Florida on the south, the finest race of men, in *physique*, in this country are to be found between the parallels of 34° and 40° north latitude, and particularly in the States of Maryland, Virginia, and Kentucky. They are large, symmetrically formed, erect and graceful in carriage, and have generally fine, open, and pleasant countenances. A newspaper correspondent, writing from the interior of Kentucky, says: "I have been struck with the profusion of really great-looking men at the State Fair. You may single out any group of twenty, and in it you will be sure to find two or three who, in stature, physical development, or expression of countenance, bear testimony to the manliness and royalty of their nature. *It seems as if Kentucky were educating a race of kings, from which to supply the world.*"

vail, often experience a marked change in their con
stitutions, the plumpness and ruddiness imparted
by the rich vital currents which flow through the
deeply-seated blood-vessels of the Englishman or
the German, giving place, in many cases, on immi-
gration to America, to denser, harder, and less rounded muscles, and a darker and less transparent complexion—in other words, a decrease of the sanguine
and nutritive and a corresponding increase of the
bilious and locomotive elements of the physical organization. If, as is often the case, the tendency in
the individual to predominant vitality is too strong
to be overcome by the external influences brought
to bear upon him here, they are pretty sure to show
their full power in his progeny, who will generally
approach the American type. In Americans, residing for a long time in England, or in any other country with a humid atmosphere, the opposite change
may take- place, the vital system becoming relatively
more influential.

Elevated situations promote the development of
bone and muscle, and therefore tend to the increase
of the motive constitution, and this change will be
greatest and most rapid where residence in mountainous regions is conjoined with all the bodily exercise and the hardships incident to mountain life,
in .its normal form. If the exercise and the hardships are not excessive, they promote a rough type
of manly beauty, but are unfavorable to the development of feminine attractiveness, and the women of
mountainous countries, such as the Highlands of
Scotland, are generally noted for their homeliness.

On the other hand, in some of the eastern countries of England, where the Vital Temperament is almost universal, and often excessively developed, the advantage in beauty is all on the side of the women, the rotund bodies and short, tapering limbs so gener-. ally prevailing, being unsuited to the male.

III.—CHANGES FROM BODILY HABITS.

Changes of occupation, general personal habits, or even of diet, often lead to important modifications of Temperament. Sedentary pursuits, even when not calling into special action the intellectual powers, tend to promote habits of reflection favorable to the development of the Mental Temperament. A change to more active outdoor employments gives the vital organs and the muscular system more relative strength and influence, and favors the predominance of one or the other. Let the shoemaker, with his slender muscles, narrow chest, and Mental Temperament, quit the bench and become a sailor, a lumberman, or a pioneer farmer in the West, and if he do not break down under the change, his chest will expand, his muscles thicken and become tough, and his digestion and all the functions of nutrition increase in activity and efficiency, while the brain, called less into action, will become comparatively quiescent, and the Mental Temperament will give place to the Motive, or the Mental-Motive. So the sailor, the lumberman, or the farmer turning shoemaker is likely to experience an equally notable change in the opposite direction.

A rich diet composed in large part of farinaceous

foods, sugar, and flesh meats fosters Alimentiveness and promotes the Vital Temperament, while a lighter diet of vegetables, fruits, eggs, and fish is favorable to the Mental Temperament. The Motive Temperament is promoted by lean meats, especially the flesh of quadrupeds, wheat-meal, corn-meal, beans, cabbages, and parsnips. It will, therefore, be apparent that changes in diet affect in a greater or less degree the balance of the constitution.

IV.—CHANGES PRODUCED BY MENTAL AGENCIES.

Geo. Combe in one of his valuable works points out the important changes produced in Temperament by a continued course of training. "It is common," he says, "for the Bilious to be changed into the Nervous Temperament by habits of mental activity and close study; and, on the other hand, we often see the Nervous or Bilious changed into the Lymphatic about the age of forty, when the nutritive system seems to acquire the preponderance." Spurzheim was accustomed to say that he had originally a large portion of the Lymphatic element, as had all his family; but that in himself the Lymphatic had gradually diminished, and the Nervous increased; whereas, in his sisters, owing to mental inactivity, the reverse had happened, and when he visited them, after being absent many years, found them, to use his own expression, "as large as tuns."

Of the wonderful influence of the mind over the body, in changing its forms and conditions, there can be no doubt. Illustrations of the effects of mental action upon the physical system abound and offer themselves to every observer. As to Temperament, De La Sarthe, in his *Traité Complet de Physiognomie*, goes so far as to assert that it is practicable, by means of an appropriate hygienic education, to develop in a child any desired constitutional condition, and that even in mature life such changes as the health and happiness of the subject may demand are effected with comparative ease; and he finds it a matter for wonder that while it is our privilege to shape at will the plastic system of the child, and in a degree of the adult also, and thus promote in the most important particulars the health, well-being, and happiness of our offspring, our friends and the world in general, that we are content to occupy ourselves, rather, in improving the breeds of our domestic animals, or in producing new and better varieties of fruits and vegetables. As an example of a change of Temperament in mature life through mental causes, he cites the case of Jean Jacques Rousseau, as follows:

" He possessed originally the Sanguine Temperament, and a character expansive, self-confident, and happy, which he retained in full activity up to the age of twenty-five. At that time he was thrown into a struggle, hostile, open, and incessant, with most of the learned societies; was made the object of reiterated attacks from antagonistic writers—enemies, some of them real enough, but a great number imaginary— and subjected to never-ceasing painful excitements, the causes of which he greatly exaggerated. Under these influences he changed by degrees, both in character and Temperament, becoming bilious, nervous, melancholic, gloomy, restless, suspicious, misanthropic, and the most unhappy of men."

Phrenologists have shown clearly enough that mental culture has power to change the form of the cranium, expanding the forehead and diminishing the lateral dimensions of the base of the brain, the organs of which are rendered less active, and held under more restraint in proportion as the intellect is developed; and it needs no proof, that whatever has power to modify the bony encasement of the brain, may modify, in at least as high a degree, the temperamental condition of the body, and consequently its configuration. The same educational influences which change the frontal lines of the head, render th)se of the body more delicate, and give the face more refinement, mobility, and expression—in short, promote the Mental Temperament, while diminishing the relative development and influence of the Motive and Vital systems. An opposite class of influences will reverse all this, and reduce the Mental, while calling out more fully the Motive and Vital forces.

"Let a well-educated person of an intellectual organization, and, to make the example as striking as possible, of mature age, be deprived of his books and intellectual companionship, thrown into the society of coarse, uneducated people; subjected to rude labor or exercise, to the almost entire exclusion of consecutive thinking; and made to adopt the gross diet which usually accompanies the other conditions we have named, and mark the result. Another set of faculties are now brought into action. The base of the brain expands; the lower features grow broader, the neck

FIG. 48.—JAMES E. MURDOCK.

FIG. 49.—HENRY IRVING.

BRAIN IN THE MOTIVE TEMPERAMENT.

PLATE XXIII.

thicker, the eyes duller, the mouth coarser, and the face, as a whole, rounder and less expressive. The whole frame shares in the degeneracy. The muscles become thicker, the joints larger, the limbs less graceful, and the body stouter and grosser." In short, the Mental predominance may be lost as well as gained, and the Motive or the Vital substituted.

These indisputable facts should be borne in mind by all, and especially by parents and teachers, as having a most important bearing upon education, both mental and physical.

JOHN GUTENBERG, INVENTOR OF PRINTING.
BRAIN IN THE MOTIVE TEMPERAMENT.

VIII.

TEMPERAMENT AND MENTALITY.

As we have said before, the primary cause of Temperament lies in the mental constitution, the body being but the external expression—the outward symbol and instrument of the mind, which fashions its temporary dwelling-place, and changes it at will, to suit its own changing character and needs. A Temperament, then, does not create or cause any particular mental characteristic or group of characteristics, but is conjoined with such characteristics because suited to their special manifestations; and being associated with them, has a tendency, by a natural reaction, to increase and perpetuate them. So Temperament becomes a sign of character, and to some extent a secondary cause of character, through the facilities it affords for the proper action of the faculties with which it is specially associated.

The student of character is, therefore, justified in making Temperament one of the first subjects of investigation, in collecting the materials for a correct estimate of the mental and moral status of an individual, and he will naturally look at it in connection with the indications afforded by the developments of the different organs of the brain, as indicated in the form of the skull. It will assist him, perhaps, if, in addition to the mental characteristics of each Tem-

FIG. 50.—J. G. BLAINE.

FIG. 51.—MADAM H. P. BLAVATSKY.

BRAIN IN THE VITAL TEMPERAMENT.

PLATE XXIV.

perament as given, in general terms, in a previous chapter, we now specify more particularly what cerebral developments accompany and give tone to each.

I.—THE BRAIN IN THE MOTIVE TEMPERAMENT
(Figs. 48 and 49).

Large Perceptive faculties, impelling to observation and fitting for the practical affairs of active life; Self-esteem, inspiring to self-reliance, aspiration, pride, and love of power; Firmness, giving tenacity of will, steadfastness, and persistent effort in any line of action determined upon; Combativeness and Destructiveness, imparting the will and ability to overcome obstacles, to resist aggression, to contend for the right, with the executive ability and the indifference to ease which permits the infliction or the endurance of the pain necessary in removing or crushing whatever may be inimical—these are some of the principal mental developments which accompany and characterize the Motive Temperament; and it is this physical constitution alone which would subserve the purposes of such a combination of mental faculties, and which, therefore, constitute at once its cause and its reason for being, while it, in turn, reacts upon the mental organization to perpetuate its peculiarities and to increase the strength and efficiency of its special powers.

Alimentiveness and Amativeness are relatively smaller than in the Vital Temperament, so that there is less liability to excesses in the direction in which they lead. Conscientiousness generally predominates over Benevolence, and Spirituality over Ideality and

6

Veneration. Hope, Mirthfulness, and Imitation are seldom either large or active.

II.—THE BRAIN IN THE VITAL TEMPERAMENT
(Figs. 50 and 51).

The mental basis and origin of the Vital Temperament lies in the base of the brain, and particularly in Alimentiveness, Acquisitiveness, and Amativeness, which are generally large, as are Benevolence, Hope, Mirthfulness, Language, and the Perceptive organs generally; but there is seldom any excessive development in any particular direction, the cranium inclining rather to roundness and evenness than to the exhibition of hollows and protuberances.

The neck being short as well as large, there is a closer communication than in the other Temperaments between the body and the brain, and a larger flow of the vital currents from the former to the latter, giving rapidity and force to the action of all the organs, but especially to those lying nearest to the source of power, in the base of the brain. It is for this reason that the animal propensities, though not relatively large perhaps, are generally so influential in persons of this constitution, and so liable, unless restrained, to hurry them into dangerous excesses.

III.—THE BRAIN IN THE MENTAL TEMPERAMENT
(Figs. 116 and 121.)

The Brain and its nervous appendages constituting the basis of the Mental Temperament, the cerebral mass, as a whole, is relatively larger in persons of this constitution than in those of either of the other

Temperaments, but this preponderance is mainly in the frontal and coronal regions—the intellectual faculties and the moral sentiments. Causality, Comparison, Ideality, Spirituality, and Veneration are generally prominent, while Combativeness, Destructiveness, Alimentiveness, Acquisitiveness, and Amativeness are not so fully developed. The real power of the intellectual faculties is not susceptible of being fully measured by their size as their activity and strength, depending in part upon a high nervous stimulus, is greater in proportion to their size in this Temperament than in the others. The quickness and clearness of the conceptions, the intensity of the emotions, and the delicacy and refinement of the taste are due as much to the texture as to the size of the organs through which these mental qualities are manifested.

In the Mental Temperament, the brain has a greater influence over the bodily conditions, as of health and disease, strength and weakness, than in the Motive or Vital Temperaments, and the mind is less dependent upon bodily states for its efficient action. It must, however, have vital power to draw upon as a reserve or its action can not be sustained. The nutritive system must, therefore, be sedulously cultivated by those who possess this constitution.

Thus we have seen that Temperament and mental character are closely correlated, and that because one has inherited or acquired a certain cerebral organization, he assumes, physically, that constitutional condition best suited to the needs of that cerebral organization, and through which its characteristic

activities may become in the highest degree affective.   The strong will; the cool, steady judgment;
the tireless energy; the indomitable courage; the
persistent purpose; the dominating ambition; the insatiable love of power; the never-failing self-reliance
of a strong executive character, require and associate
with themselves the Motive Temperament. Vivacity;
versatility; impulse; ardor; love of pleasure; desire for change; fondness for good living; intellectual
quickness and brilliancy; instability of purpose; and
amiability and genial kindliness could find no adequate expression in any other than the Vital Temperament. The predominating intellectuality, taste,
refinement, lofty aspirations, intense emotions, and
clear, vivid conceptions of the literary, artistic, and
imaginative organization are fitly embodied in the
fine, sensitive, mobile Mental Temperament.   In
either case, it is the character or mental constitution
which comes first (by inheritance or by acquisition),
and the physical condition which follows and adapts
itself to the mind's requirements, reacting in turn
upon the latter to promote its proper action and
perpetuate and increase its special qualities.

FIG. 52.—BELVA A. LOCKWOOD.

FIG. 53.—REV. CHARLES KINGSLEY.

BRAIN IN THE MENTAL TEMPERAMENT.

PLATE XXV.

IX.

AGE AND SEX IN TEMPERAMENT.

IN treating of Changes of Temperament in a previous chapter, we have incidentally indicated some of the points in which the different periods of life affect the Temperaments; but the subject requires further elucidation, and we therefore revert to it here.

I.—THE TEMPERAMENT OF CHILDHOOD (Fig. 54).

During infancy, growth is the grand object which Nature has in view, and while she does not neglect to develop slowly the lobes of the brain, and to lay the foundation for the solid framework of bones, muscles, and ligaments, which is destined to sustain and move the body, she wisely gives her special attention to the nutritive system, as the one which should predominate in development, activity, and influence. The infant, therefore, has, normally, the Vital Temperament, the Motive and Mental systems being manifest only in a rudimentary condition; and, the diet being milk and other soft and watery aliments, it is, at first, the lymphatic element of the constitution which naturally predominates, the sanguine gaining the ascendency after a change of diet and the exercise of the limbs and body have given the respiratory and arterial systems a greater development and a more powerful influence.

We may say, then, in general terms, that the Temperament of infancy is the Vital, the lymphatic element being predominant at the outset, or during the first two or three years of life, but gradually giving place to the sanguine. The Mental system should be held in comparative abeyance during the first seven years of life at least, great care being taken that while its healthy activity is not shackled, there be no abnormal or forced and sickly development, at the expense of the physical system and the general health and symmetry of the organization. The locomotive system, in those who have inherited a tendency to the Motive Temperament, assuming year by year increased influence, normally attains ascendency at puberty.

We have been speaking of what we believe to be the order of Nature and the requirement of the law of development in the human being; but we are aware that the hereditary influences of our age and country in which there is so much feverish mental activity and such intensity of feeling and passion, with too little vital power and strength of constitution to give endurance and insure sustained effort, are not calculated to insure in American children the desired orderly development. The Mental system, obeying the strong inherited tendency, aided by a competitive and too stimulating system of education, comes early into the ascendency, dwarfing the body, and finally starving itself, by drying up, prematurely, the vital currents which should sustain it in permanent and increasing efficiency till old age.

II.— THE TEMPERAMENT OF MIDDLE AGE.
(Fig. 55).

At the age of from forty to forty-five—earlier in some and later in others—the activity of both mind and body having somewhat abated, and the passions become more cool and moderate, where sound health and a good digestion favor it, there is generally a more or less marked accession of development and activity in the nutritive system, sometimes giving a decided predominance to the Vital system in constitutions previously Motive or Mental.

Were sound health and correct habits universal, perhaps there would be no exceptions to the change we have here indicated, and the Temperament of middle age would always be either Vital or one of the Compound Temperaments formed by it with either the Motive or the Mental; but where the digestion has become impaired, or where there is a controlling necessity for an activity of body or mind no longer natural to the organization, the normal modification fails to take place, and the existing constitutional condition is rather increased than diminished, as seen in persons subjected to severe manual labor, harassed by the cares and anxieties of business, or overtaxed by close and continued intellectual effort. If, as perhaps we may say should be the case, where the road to competence and ease is open to all, the age of forty finds a man relieved from pecuniary anxieties and the necessity of labor or application to business for the support of himself and family, and can throw off or transfer to others

all the heavier burdens of life, and 'give himself
leisure for recreation and repose, we generally observe a filling up and rounding out of the contours of
the body, and the assumption of a degree of portli-
ness which is naturally associated with good health,
good living, and an easy life.

In women, this accession of vital development
would be more general were they more healthy, but,
in this country at least, their health is too often so
broken down before the " turn of life " that the *embonpoint* which properly belongs to them is lost in
a sickly emaciation. In England, where the habits
of women, as well as the climate, are more favorable,
they may look forward to the time when they shall be
" Fat, fair, and forty," and be thankful if they escape
being obese, red-faced, and coarse, as is the tendency
of their Temperament.

III.—THE TEMPERAMENT OF OLD AGE (Fig. 56).

With the more or less imperfect nutrition of old
age, there supervenes a shrinkage of bone, muscle,
and especially of cellular tissue, giving the wrinkles
which indicate and symbolize the decline of life. The
shrinkage being greatest in the softer parts, which had
previously given fullness to the form and roundness
to the cheek, the indications of the Motive Temperament are increased, though the increase of the locomotive apparatus is merely relative, and owing to the
decreased volume and activity of the nutritive system.
In this way, a Temperament which may have been
Mental-Vital, may become, through the decadence
of the vital powers, Mental-Motive, without any increase of the Motive element.

In some constitutions, as has been said in a previous chapter, the Vital system, previously strong and active, falls, on the approach of old age, into an abnormal condition, in which there is conjoined with a loss of activity in the arterial system, a clogging of the general circulation, and a repletion of the watery fluids in the cellular tissues and under the skin, giving the soft, flabby appearance seen in the Lymphatic Temperament. This constitutional condition is far more common in low, moist regions—like Holland, for instance—than in our drier climate, and is by no means infrequent in England, where the Vital Temperament is more common, and more subject to deterioration in the way indicated, than with us.

IV.—THE TEMPERAMENTS IN WOMEN.

There is no particular Temperament which belongs exclusively to woman, and no one from which she is excluded by reason of sex; but at the same time, there are certain constitutional conditions which seem peculiarly adapted to her requirements, and certain others which are clearly inconsistent with her highest adaptation to the distinctive offices of the sex.

In woman the trunk is longer in proportion to the whole stature and to the arms and legs, than in man, giving relatively more room for the development of the vital system, so essential to her, not merely for her own well-being, but for the proper performance of her offices as a mother. We may say, therefore, that the natural temperamental condition of woman is one in which the vital or nutritive element is

6*

strongly influential, if not predominant — say the Vital, Vital-Mental or Mental-Vital Temperament.

The Motive Temperament, in its typical form, is not well suited to woman, as it involves too much hardness, angularity, and harshness; but when modi-fied by a nearly equal proportion of the Vital ele-ment, to fill out the depressions and round the contours, and a good Mental development, to soften the expression and refine the prominent, but clear-cut features, there is often a high order of beauty developed, conjoined with great strength of character and high intellectual endowments.

The purely Mental Temperament, so common among the women of our age, and especially of our country, gives us beautiful girls, charming in their grace, refinement, and intelligence, but too frail, in many cases, for the practical uses of life, and doomed to premature invalidism and early death. If one could choose his own mother, he would not, if well instructed in physiology, select one of these too in-tellectual women, however lovely. With the vital element nearly equal to the mental, or at least strongly influential, there is a foundation for a char-acter at once womanly, refined, intelligent, amiable, and warm-hearted.

That morbid condition described in the old classi-fication as the Nervous Temperament, is, unfortu-nately, very common among women of low vitality, especially when they are addicted to strong tea and coffee, late hours, and the fashionable dissipations of the day.

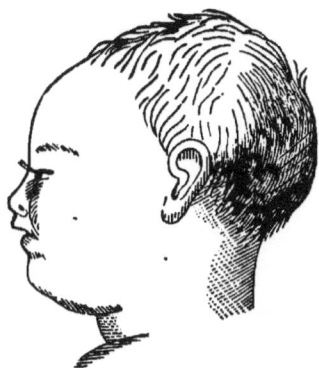

FIG. 54.—CHILDHOOD.

FIG. 55.—MIDDLE AGE.
BISHOP LYNCH.

FIG. 56.—OLD AGE.   A. B. ALCOTT.

AGE AND TEMPERAMENT.

PLATE XXVI.

FIG. 57.—CHARLES ALGERNON SWINBURNE.

FIG. 58.—CROWN PRINCESS OF GERMANY.

TEMPERAMENT IN MARRIAGE.

PLATE XXVII.

X.

TEMPERAMENT IN THE DOMESTIC RELATIONS.

In the relations of human beings to each other in society, there prevail certain laws of harmony analogous to those which govern the combination of the various notes in music. We strike certain keys simultaneously and there is produced a pleasing accordance 'of sweet sounds. Those keys represent notes bearing a harmonic relation to each other—they form chords. Other notes, each equally sweet in itself, sounded together, strike the ear dissonantly. In a like manner, we may bring together two or more persons, standing in certain natural constitutional relations to each other, and there will at once ensue mutual likings, sympathy, and friendship, or love, while the same persons, or others not less amiable and lovable, transposed into other combinations, may simply make each other miserable; and the closer the connection, the more cruelly will they torture each other.

With these harmonies and discords in human relations, and especially those of the family, Temperament has much to do, and those sustaining or purposing to assume such relations should study well the laws of mental and temperamental consonance, so that life-music and not an infernal jarring of dissonant individualities may be the result of the union. We do not dream of becoming successful performers

on the piano or the organ, without a fair knowledge
of the science of music; much less should we presume
to deal with the profounder harmonies of humanity,
in ignorance of the laws in accordance with which
men and women are constituted complements of each
other, or fitted to assume places as components of
a chord in social life.

I.—TEMPERAMENT AND MATRIMONY.

In marriage, above all other relations in life, harmonious conditions are essential.   Not only the
happiness of the parties originally concerned are involved, but the physical symmetry, mental balance,
and general well-being of offspring also.   The conse-
quences of a discordant union may involve many
generations in misery, or—a less melancholy fate—
result in the extinction of a family.

Some physiologists have taught that the constitutions of the parties in marriage should be similar, so
as to insure similar tastes, habits, and modes of
thought, while others have contended that contrasts
should be sought, to give room for variety and prevent the stagnation of a level sameness.   Neither of
these statements expresses fully the true law of selection, though both are partly true.   There can be no
harmony without a difference, but there may be difference without harmony.   It is not because she is
like him that a man loves a woman, but because she
is unlike.   For the same reason she loves him.   The
qualities which the one lacks are those which in the
other attract and hold the fancy and the heart.   The
more womanly the woman, the greater her power

over men, and in proportion as she approaches the
masculine in person or in character will she repel the
other sex; while a woman admires, no less, in man
true manliness, and feels for effeminacy and weakness
in him either pity or contempt. What should be
sought and what is sought, as a rule, in a husband or
a wife, where arbitrary conventional customs and
considerations of rank, wealth, and position are not
allowed to interfere, is not a counterpart, but a complement—something to supply a lack—the other self,
which shall round out one's being and form a perfect,
symmetrical whole. As in music it is not contiguous
notes which combine to form chords, but those separated from each other, as a first and a third or a third
and a fifth; so we produce social and domestic harmony by associating *graduated differences.* Two
persons may be "too much alike to agree." They
crowd each other, for "two objects can not occupy
the same space at the same time." So while a
"union of opposites" is by no means to be insisted
upon, or even recommended, as a rule, yet a too
close similarity in constitution should be avoided, as
detrimental to offspring as well as inimical to the happiness of the parties themselves. The Mental Temperament, for instance, strongly developed in both
would tend to intensify the intellectual activity, already perhaps too great, in each, and if offspring
should unfortunately result, they would be likely to
inherit in still greater excess the constitutional tendencies of the parents. In the same way, a marked
preponderance of the Motive or the Vital systems in
both parents leads to a similar state of connubial

discord, and a lack of temperamental balance in the children, if any, resulting from the union. Where there is a close approximation to a symmetrical and harmonious development—"a balance of Temperaments"—the union of similar organizations is less objectionable and may result favorably, as respects both parents and children; but such cases are so rare that a rule drawn from them would prove of little practical value.

The disastrous effects upon their offspring of the marriage of blood relations, it seems probable, are mainly, if not wholly, referable to the similarity of constitution inherited by each from the common stock; for we find that such unions are by no means uniformly unfavorable to progeny—some instances being quoted by eminent writers on the subject, where intermarriage has resulted in the improvement instead of the deterioration of the families' thus uniting their members. It is likely that a close investigation into the circumstances in such cases would show either an approximate balance of temperamental elements in the parties, furnishing no excesses or deficiencies to be exaggerated in progeny, or else an exceptional diversity in the constitutions of the male and female members of these families.

The Vital system is the life-giving and life-sustaining element in the human constitution, and must be considered as the physical basis of marriage and of parentage. This temperamental element should therefore, undoubtedly be strongly indicated in one, at least, of the parties to a conjugal union; and if strikingly deficient in one, should be predominant in

FIG. 59.—MISS ———.

FIG. 60.—VICTOR M. RICE.

TEMPERAMENT AND MARRIAGE.

PLATE XXVIII.

the other, to insure a proper balance in offspring. A man like Fig. 57, for instance, with an excess of the Mental Temperament and deficient in vital stamina, should either remain single or marry a woman organized like Fig. 58 or Fig. 66, with an immense fund of vitality, but sufficiently intellectual to appreciate him, share, in a degree, his aspirations and sympathize with him in his tastes. With one like Fig. 59 for a wife, the children, if any, would probably be few and puny and die young, the too keen sensibilities, the excess of mental activity, and the intensity of all the pains they suffer or the pleasures they enjoy, would soon wear out the inadequate physical system with which alone their parents were able to endow them.

Where the Motive Temperament is strongly indicated, as in Figs. 64 and 65, there is needed in the one selected as " partner for life," a predominance of the vital or nutritive system, as in Figs. 62 and 66, to impart vivacity and cheerfulness to the family circle, and to transmit to offspring the proper degree of mental and physical activity, warmth, amiability, and suavity of character, as well as to give a desirable softness and plumpness to the physical system ; while a good development of the Mental is requisite to refine, elevate, stimulate, and give intellectual power and æsthetic tastes.

A man with a strongly developed Motive Temperament (Figs. 64 and 65), united in marriage to a woman of the same organization (Fig. 63), would lack the stimulating, warming, and softening influences which so favorably modify the somewhat slow, cold, rough,

hard, and austere features characteristic of the constitution, and the pair would move too slowly for the
current of progress around them, unless awakened
by the strong influence of some grand revolutionary
movement, and their children would inherit, in a still
higher degree, their homely angularities of person,
and their energetic, persistent, and sturdy, but hard,
rough, and severe traits of character. Fortunately
the Motive Temperament (Fig. 63) is not a common
one among women, nor do men of this organization
affect their style of beauty, even in its modified
feminine form, but look rather for the plump rosiness
of the fair-haired blonde, or the pale, delicate loveli-
ness of the gray-eyed Psyche, whose frailness appeals
to their strength, and whose mental quickness contrasts so strongly with their slow, but powerful intellectual movements. In general, a medium between
these two attractions will be found the safest and best
course for them.

A rational, natural, and harmonious marriage connection requires to have its foundations laid in a
broad, full vitality, but this element must not comprise also the superstructure. Where both parties
are of the Vital Temperament (Figs. 60 and 66), the
union is not favorable, either to them or to their
children. There being no cooling, restraining, or refining influence at work with them, the parents are
apt to give way too much to their impulses and passions, to live too fast, to fall into excesses and dissipations, be fitful, vacillating, and indolent, and to
transmit to their children too much of the animal
nature, too little mental power, and an excess of

FIG. 61.—HON. MR. JULIAN

FIG. 62.—PRINCESS GISELA OF AUSTRIA.

TEMPERAMENT AND MARRIAGE.

PLATE XXIX.

appetite, passion, and love of pleasure. An influential development of the Mental and the Motive (Figs. 59 and 65) elements in a husband or wife should be sought by a person of a full Vital Temperament (Figs. 58 and 60), the one to give toughness, consistency, persistence, and coolness, and the other to refine and elevate the character, and impart intellectuality, taste, and love of culture to offspring.

From the foregoing considerations it appears that the point to be aimed at is a proper balance in all the temperamental elements, what is lacking in the husband to be made up by the wife, and *vice versa*— the one being a complement or counterpoise of the other, so that an even development, as nearly as possible, may be transmitted to offspring.

Beyond the somewhat general statements thus made, the correctness of which can hardly be called in question, it is not, perhaps, in the present state of our knowledge of the laws of social harmony, safe to go. We have correctly given, as we believe, the general law of harmony in our social relations. If we can not lay down exact formula for its practical application, which will apply to all cases, it is simply because the gamut of the human passions, unlike that of the musical notes, has not been definitely determined, or the elements of our physical organization reduced to a graduated series. The time will come, in the progress of the race in knowledge, when men will touch with no uncertain fingers the keys which are to render the sublime anthem of disenthralled and harmonized humanity. In the meantime, reader, first " know thyself," mentally and tem-

peramentally, and then, through the "Signs of
Character"—as stamped upon every organization—
upon the cranium, upon the face, upon every organ,
feature, and movement—study and become acquainted with those around you, and you will find
little difficulty in determining, in reference to any
particular individual of the opposite sex, whether
there is between you and him or her that *graduated
difference* which might bring harmony out of union.

II.—Temperament and Family Government.

As some of the children resemble the father, others
"take after" the mother, and a third class combine
in different degrees the Temperaments of both, there
are often in the same family a diversity of organizations to deal with. The light already thrown upon
the subject, in previous chapters, will suggest a mode
of family government which shall be flexible enough
to admit of a different treatment for different organizations.

At first, as we have shown, the Vital system has
normally the ascendency in the child, and the restless activity which impels to fun and mischief, and
keeps body and limbs in perpetual motion, are but
the expression of that organic condition, and is seldom punishable, in any form, and least of all by
imprisonment—the greatest of cruelties in such cases.
If it be necessary that the child be kept still at all,
the periods of enforced quiet should be as brief as
possible. Whether one may "spare the rod" and
not "spoil the child" or not, is a question we do not
purpose to discuss here; but a little whipping, if it

FIG. 63.—LOLA MONTEZ.

FIG. 64.—A. E. B. PHELPS.

TEMPERAMENT IN MARRIAGE.

PLATE XXX.

do no good, will do no great harm to a child of the Vital Temperament, and will soon be forgotten, as well as the occasion which called for it.

When the Mental Temperament becomes influential, as it unfortunately too often does at an early age in those who have inherited a strong tendency to it, the keen sensibilities, the refined tastes, the self-respect, the sense of moral responsibility, give the parent something higher than fear of the rod to which he can appeal, and make corporal punishments degrading as well as cruel. The basis of parental government is then entirely changed and placed on a higher plane. Children prematurely developed in the intellectual faculties and in the moral sentiments, require little correction of any kind. They are generally "good little boys and girls," who are pointed out by parents and teachers as examples for those embodiments of fun and mischief, the robust, full-blooded, round-faced "children who will be children," and act like children, in spite of both precept and example to the contrary. If "whom the gods love die young," their affections are evidently given to the "smart" juvenile men and women, who love their books, do not care for play, and are too good to require the rod. Parents love them too, and if they desire to keep them on earth for the performance of their life's work here, they should restrain their too great mental activity, and encourage exercise and active sports, and foster in every possible way the development of the Vital system.

The Motive Temperament is less liable than the Mental to premature development. It sometimes, however, makes its physical and mental peculiarities manifest at too early a day. Children of this Temperament have not the bodily activity and love of motion characteristic of those in whom the Vital system predominates, or the intellectual liveliness and quickness of those possessing the Mental Temperament. They are strong and tough, but deliberate in movement and in thought, and may seem dull and stupid by the side of those in whom brain-power is the leading element, but they have stamina, steadiness, energy, and perseverance, and are not unlikely to reach the distant goal ahead of their more active competitors. They are not so apt to "get into scrapes," or to transgress the rules, through a mere thoughtless love of mischief, as those having the Vital constitution, but they do not like to be subjected to authority, and are often rebellious against wholesome restraint, while their strong wills, dogged resolutions, pluck, and persistency render them very difficult to manage. They must be held in with a taut rein and a strong hand. No compromises or half-way measures will do for them. They will give up only when their slow-acting, but cool and correct judgment tells them that it would be folly to resist.

III.—ILLUSTRATIVE EXAMPLES.

When it comes to dealing with daughters of a marriageable age, but still "infants" in the eyes of the law, a most delicate and often difficult task is imposed upon parents. Having watched over, nursed, and educated them with a tender solicitude for their welfare, and seen them grow up in beauty and moral love-

FIG. 65.—R. B. WOODWARD.

FIG. 66.—NELL GWYNNE.

TEMPERAMENT AND MARRIAGE.

PLATE XXXI

liness, it is hard sometimes to give them up, even to the most honorable, suitable, and loving husband; and sometimes the suitor is not suitable, and there is reason to believe that the union on which the daughter has set her heart would prove disastrous to her happiness. What shall the devoted parents do? The author of " Wedlock "* answers this momentous question in the light of Temperament and Mental Organization by means of the following illustrative examples, which we can do no better than to quote in full :

THE CASE OF MARY SMITH.

Mary Smith is a young lady of sixteen summers, living in the country. She has a predominance of the Vital Temperament, average intelligence and moral sense, moderate Self-esteem and Firmness, and pretty strong social feelings. She is fashionably rather than solidly educated, and is vivacious, affectionate, amiable, and easily influenced by stronger and more positive natures—a good girl, but one with no great strength either of character or feeling. Her future will depend far more upon others than upon herself.

Mary goes to the city to visit some relatives, and is thrown into the society of a number of young men. One of them—a dark-haired, muscular man, with a predominating Motive Temperament, and a strong, positive, imperious character—pays her particular attentions, says pleasant things, and makes

---

* Wedlock; or, The Right Relation of the Sexes. New York S. R. Wells & Co.

himself generally agreeable. He dresses well, sings delightfully, and has all the external polish of a gentleman. His person and manners please Mary's Ideality, and his attentions (something new to her) gratify her Approbativeness; and when he says he loves her, she thinks herself very much in love with him. He visits her in the country. Mr. Smith don't like him. He has more knowledge of men than his daughter. We will not suppose him to be either a phrenologist or a physiognomist, but he has an intuitive perception of character, and the young man's looks do not please him. He makes inquiries in the city, and learns that this candidate for his daughter's hand is a "fast" young man of a decidedly dissolute character.

Now when this *roué* "proposes" and is referred to "pa," what shall Mr. Smith do? Shall he allow his daughter to throw herself away upon this miserable scamp, whom she thinks she loves, but whom she would soon, if married to him, learn to despise and loathe? The father says *No*, very emphatically; and he does right. The young man storms, and Miss Mary cries and declares in the most positive manner that she can never live without her dear Harry—that all her hopes of happiness in this world are nipped in the bud, and much more of the same sort, in all of which she is perfectly sincere. It grieves her good father to be obliged to distress her, but he knows too much of her character to have any fears of permanent ill-effects from her disappointment.

Within a year the "dear Harry" has eloped with a Madison-Square heiress, and Mary has another

FIG. 67.—HORACE A. BUTTOLPH.

FIG. 68.—MARIE SOPHIE SCHWARTZ.

TEMPERAMENT IN THE TEACHER.

PLATE XXXII.

lover, and is as smiling and happy as ever. She has long since thanked her father, with tears of gratitude in her eyes, for having saved her from the selfish adventurer whom she thought she loved.

This was a "love affair," in the common acceptation of the term, but there was really no true love concerned in it. On one side it was a heartless and selfish piece of deception, and on the other a mere passing fancy. Similar cases are constantly occurring, and the duty of parents in reference to them, it seems to us, is plain. Remember Mr. Smith, and go and do likewise.

Now let us look at a case of another kind:

ELLEN JONES' "LOVE AFFAIR."

Ellen Jones is in many respects the opposite of Mary Smith. A Mental-Motive Temperament; a good degree of Self-esteem and Firmness, with not too much Approbativeness; considerable Combativeness and strong affections give her mental constitution a marked and decided character. She is not easily led, and has a mind and a will of her own. She, moreover, is nineteen; has been a good deal in "society;" has had suitors; and is accustomed to the polite attentions of gentlemen, which she knows how to estimate at their proper value.

At last Ellen finds herself loved by one whose love she can return; and she loves him with all the ardor and strength of her strong, positive nature. He is adapted to her in Temperament and disposition, and loves her truly; but in this case, as in the other, the father does not approve of the daughter's choice

Nothing can be said against the young man's moral character; but he is poor; is not, in Mr. Jones' opinion, calculated to make a fortune very soon; and in social position is not Ellen's equal. Mr. Jones thinks Ellen might do better—a *great deal* better.

Will Mr. Jones imitate Mr. Smith, and put his veto on the engagement? Not if he be wise and love his daughter. He has no soft, pliable, easy nature to deal with. When Ellen says she loves, she knows what she is talking about, and means all she says; and if she declare that a union with the chosen one is absolutely essential to her happiness, she states merely the simple fact. To love once, with her, is to love forever. If her father refuse his consent, she will wait till of age and then marry, if need be, *without* his consent; or if he succeed in breaking off the match altogether, he will have blighted his daughter's life and destroyed her only chance for happiness in this world. He should yield to her wishes even against his own judgment in regard to the fitness of the match.

This is also a sample of a large class of cases in which we think the duty of parents is equally plain as in the other. Any interference that shall amount to a prohibition can result in nothing but evil. It is best, when dealing with such characters and under such circumstances, to let love take its course even though we can not fully approve its choice.

There are cases, no doubt, hardly referable to either of these classes, in which it will be exceedingly difficult to decide rightly what to do—cases to which no general rule that we can lay down will apply; but a knowledge of the human organization, physical and mental, a conscientious desire to do right, and an humble reliance upon Divine guidance, will generally make plain the path of duty in this as in other matters involving human feelings and human welfare.

WENDELL PHILLIPS.

7

XI.

TEMPERAMENT AND EDUCATION.

In both the teacher and the pupil, Temperament is an element of no small importance. If the one is to impart knowledge, draw out latent powers, and develop natural capacities, he must not merely have the knowledge to impart and be aware of the existence of the powers and capacities upon which he is to operate, but he must understand the physical and mental organization of the subject of his efforts, in order to know how best to open his mind and throw the vivifying light into its inmost recesses; and if the other is to receive knowledge, to give out his latent powers, and grow in understanding and capacity for the conception of ideas, he must be placed under conditions suited to his peculiar constitution and favorable to his natural activity. In other words, the teacher must have aptness to teach and the pupil must be placed in conditions of temperamental harmony with his teacher and with his fellow-students; and this implies, on the part of the former, a suitable Temperament in himself, and a good, practical knowledge of the doctrine of the Temperaments, to be applied in the labors of the school-room—in classifying his pupils, in suiting his instructions to the various classes, and in governing widely different dispositions.

I.—TEMPERAMENT IN THE TEACHER (Figs. 67 and 68).

Physically, the good teacher must have vital stamina, toughness, and endurance; mentally, he must be active, clear-headed, and comprehensive; morally, he must be warm-hearted, sympathetic, and affable, as well as energetic, persevering, and firm. There must be a sufficient development of the Motive constitution to give strength and density of fiber to the body, and coolness, steadfastness, and force of character to the mind; enough of the Mental element to impart delicacy, refinement, intellectual quickness, capacity, and high moral principles; and so much of the Vital condition as will serve to sustain and give vigor, warmth, susceptibility, and vivacity to both the physical and the mental functions. In short, the teacher requires, as near as may be, a balance of the temperamental elements. With such an organization—too rare, we fear, at present, to supply all the teachers the world needs—there will be dignity without stiffness; determination without harshness; liveliness without frivolity; pluck and executive power without quarrelsomeness; ardor and enthusiasm without passion and blind impulse; and capacity for conception and expression without pedantry and volubility. He would not only possess the necessary knowledge, but would be able to communicate it; not only have the capacity to lead, but the power to control; and he would be loved as well as respected.

Without an approximation to the qualifications we have enumerated, no one is or can be fitted for the

office of teacher, though where persons suitably or
ganized and educated can not be found, we must, of
course, do the best we can with the inferior materials
at command. Where the natural educator, with all
the acquired qualifications which study and experience can impart, offers himself, he should be gladly
received, duly honored, and adequately rewarded; so
that he will not be tempted to seek some other
profession because more remunerative or more respected. Of all who aspire to teach, it should at
least be required that they have a practical knowledge of the Temperaments and the ability to adapt
their instructions, in a degree at least, to the organization of each class of pupils.

II.—TEMPERAMENT IN THE PUPIL (Figs. 69 to 72).

With a classification of pupils according to Temperament, practicable and easy with him, the properly
organized and qualified teacher, having, as nearly as
may be, a balanced Temperament, would be able to
put himself, through his sympathy and adaptability,
into intimate relations with each class, on its own
plane. The intellectual activity and studiousness of
the Mental; the slowness, but effective power and
persistence of the Motive; and the liveliness, susceptibility, and instability of the Vital, would all be met
with a wise forethought of each temperamental pecu-
liarity, and the mode of instruction and of discipline
adapted to each in turn.

1. *The Mental Temperament* (Fig. 69).—Children in
whom the Mental system is most influential are disposed to intellectual activity, have desire to learn.

FIG. 69.—MENTAL TEMPERAMENT.

FIG. 70.—MOTIVE TEMPERAMENT.

FIG. 71.—VITAL TEMPERAMENT

FIG. 72.—VITAL TEMPERAMENT.

TEMPERAMENT IN CHILDREN.

PLATE XXXIII.

and acquire knowledge rapidly. They are generally fond of study, have excellent memories for facts and rules, and readily comprehend the teacher's explanations, where any are required. They go to the head of their classes, get much praise for their studiousness and their remarkable proficiency in their studies, and are incited thereby to still greater exertions. They need no stimulus to quicken their attention or spur them on, but, on the contrary, often require to be held back, and the counteracting influences of occupations and recreations, involving outdoor muscular exercise, brought to bear upon them to prevent permanent injury to their physical constitutions. They should be encouraged to frequent the gymnasium (if one be at hand under proper physiological management), to play ball, to row, and to ride. Explain to them, good teacher (and they will readily understand you), that without health and vital stamina their learning will avail them nothing in the end, and that they, proud as they are of their superior attainments, will finally be distanced in the race by the dull, backward, homely fellows whose places are now at the foot of the class, unless they can acquire and retain the necessary bodily vigor to back up their mental activity.

Fig. 69 is that of an intellectually precocious boy, and examples of a similar configuration are, alas! too common. It is the body, in such cases, rather than the mind, which needs culture, and we beg the parents and teachers of such children, as they value their health, their welfare—their lives, in fact—to cease to stimulate their minds and hasten to pro-

mote vital and muscular development, as a means
of imparting an enduring power to the brain, as well
as of counteracting its excessive activity. It is sometimes said of such children that they are "old-look-
ing," and the remark is a correct one. Such a form
of head and face belongs only to the adult, and is a
deformity in a child. Children of such an organization and configuration are "too smart to live;" and,
if they do not die young, will fail to realize the fond
hopes of their parents, simply on account of the lack
of physical power.

2. *The Vital Temperament* (Figs. 71 and 72).—Here
we find activity equal to that manifested in the
Mental Temperament, but it is of another kind, and
leads to different results. Children of the Vital
Temperament (sanguine type) are round-faced, ruddy,
blue-eyed, light-haired, overflowing with animal spirits, perpetually in motion, full of jollity and good
nature, prone to mischief, and not very fond of either
study or hard work. Their attention is easily at-
tracted, however, and though it can be held but a
short time to any particular subject, they learn
readily, provided the lessons be made easy and not
too long. They are always wide awake, listen eagerly
when the teacher speaks, and like to get their instruction orally, instead of from the text-book; but
in any case their attention is as easily diverted as it
is gained, and long-continued application is impossible. Such children require frequent recesses for
recreation, and should be allowed some latitude in
the way of movement in the school-room. They
can not be kept still, and all attempts to enforce the

law of quietness must end in failure. Mr. Sizer, in the *American Phrenological Journal*, recommends to classify such children together, if possible, and " once in twenty minutes have them march around the room ; let them study standing for five minutes, and then sitting; let one of them listen to the lesson of the others, and alternate ; they should have stories told ; they should recite in concert, so that they may have a chance to make a noise. In short, every method should be devised to give them occasion for change. These children have generally a good memory of words ; they will learn to recite by heart;ʻ they are good spellers, often have a talent for figures, and are very fond of geography, though they would like to study by taking the world for a map." They will be rather superficial at best, but will make the most in after-life of all the knowledge they may acquire. For abstract science, thorough investigation, and patient research, they have neither the taste nor the capacity.

Children in whom the dark variety of the Vital Temperament (Bilious-Vital) prevails, while manifesting a similar restless activity of body, love of fun and mischief, impatience of restraint, and distaste for hard study, lack the alertness and impressibility of the sanguine variety. On the contrary, they are apt to be rather dull, slow, inert, and passive, as regards the reception of instruction; but they are more persistent in their attention and application, and have more retentive memories, offering a firmer basis for judicious culture than the other class. They are stronger-willed and more passionate and obstinate than children of the light-haired type.

3. *The Motive Temperament* (Fig. 70).—As we have elsewhere shown, the Motive Temperament is not a normal one in childhood and early youth, the Vital system naturally predominating. It is, however, sometimes, though much less frequently than the Mental constitution, prematurely developed, particularly in respect to those characteristics which are due to the influence of the Bilious element. It becomes necessary, therefore, to deal with it in the family and the school, much more frequently than might, at the first view, be inferred; and often in the persons of boys and girls (but more particularly the former) who manifest in their configuration and general appearance but few of its physical traits. Its homely prominences and angularities come later.

The child in whom the bilious element is predominant, and who is, by inheritance, strongly predisposed to the full development of the Motive or Muscular Temperament, will be slow and dull as a student, receiving impressions with difficulty and requiring much explanation and illustration, to enable him to comprehend and fully appropriate the instruction; but whatever is acquired, is retained with great tenacity, ånd each fact or principle mastered is an entering wedge which tends to open the mind to further acquirements. There is no brilliancy about him, but he is sound, practical, and strong. If the superstructure goes up slowly and roughly, it has at least a solid foundation and a promise of enduring stability. It requires unselfish devotion as well as patience and perseverance, on the part of the teacher, to do justice to the pupil who manifests so little aptness, and who makes no show of extraordinary progress to give *éclat* to examination day; but the time may come when, after all his brilliant pupils shall have passed into commonplace men and women and been forgotten, he will be proud in saying: " He was my pupil. I gave his mind its early discipline, and drew out, by dint of persistent effort, his latent capacities."

Daniel Webster was one of those slow, backward boys, of whom little is expected, but who by and by astonish the world by their exhibition of strength of mind and executive ability. He had not the Motive Temperament, but possessed that less common combination of the bilious with the vital constitution, which gives in childhood and youth a similar mental inertness and passivity, but which, later in life, when the brain has come to be more fully developed and ambition has been awakened, becomes a source of power, stability, and enduring efficiency.

The grand object, in dealing with children of the Motive Temperament, is to awaken the slumbering energies of the mind, by bringing to bear upon them the stimulus of emulation among those of similar organization, and by pointing out to them examples in history which shall excite their ambition and encourage their hopes. Above all, have patience with them and do not set them down as dunces because they lack quickness and brilliancy. If sufficient mental development and activity can be secured, they will, in the end, take their places as leaders in the spheres of active life; otherwise, they will be fitted only for the world's rough, hard work, or for the still rougher ways of lawlessness, violence, and

7*

crime. They do not like restraint, and, both as children and as men, are often inclined to be insubordi-
nate and set law and order at defiance. Firmness and
inflexibility, tempered with kindness, should be exercised in their discipline.

III.—GENERAL CONSIDERATIONS.

How far it may be practicable, at present, to
classify the children in our public or private schools
on the basis of temperamental organization, we are
not prepared to say, but we are confident that this
is a result to be desired and prepared for, and sure
to be reached, sooner or later, as enlightened views
of the human organization shall generally prevail.
Without this classification, however, a knowledge of
the facts we have briefly set forth will enable the intelligent teacher to adapt his instructions and discipline in some degree to the natural disposition of
each pupil. He will give the studious, sharp-witted,
clear-headed subjects of the Mental Temperament
no long and minute explanations of rules or principles, which they grasp at once, from their books, but
will lead their minds rather to the practical applica-
tions of these rules and principles, which they are
liable to overlook, and to the danger of excessive
mental activity, in connection with defective vitality;
to the impulsive, ardent, versatile, vivacious, and volatile pupils whom the rich, warm blood of the Vital
Temperament impels to perpetual action, he will
prescribe short lessons, frequent changes, and abundant recreation, without attempting to chain their
roving minds continuously to any one subject; while

the stronger, but slower and less impressible "dark, homely, bilious fellows" will be patiently drilled according to the deliberate action of their own minds, clear and full explanations being alternated with time to think out the relations of things as involved in their lessons.

The different combinations of these primary Temperaments will, of course, require modifications of treatment, which will suggest themselves to the teacher who has mastered the distinctions we have so carefully indicated in previous chapters; and it should be his aim to so train the minds and bodies of the plastic beings under his charge, as to promote a harmonious blending of the temperamental elements, cultivating those which are too feebly developed and restraining and counteracting those which are too strong and active.

XII

TEMPERAMENT AND OCCUPATION.

In every profession and occupation we may find all the Temperaments represented. There are clergymen of the Vital and Motive as well as of the Mental Temperament, and sailors, soldiers, and lumbermen of the Mental and Vital as well as of the Motive Temperament; but this merely illustrates the well-known fact that people are often out of place—the round pegs in the square holes and the square pegs in the round holes—in other words, that accidental circumstances, and not scientific principles, have generally governed in the selection of a trade or profession. It is none the less true that, while some persons, by virtue of a many-sided, symmetrical, harmonious organization, are fitted to fill, with nearly equal advantage, almost any position in life, or follow any trade or profession, the vast majority is made up of those whom Nature has adapted to particular callings, by giving them organizations better suited to some particular species of activity than to others. It is the object of' this chapter to point out these adaptations, so far, at least, as they may depend upon temperamental conditions and the mental manifestations which attend and mark these conditions.

(156)

I.—ADAPTATIONS OF THE MOTIVE TEMPERAMENT
(Fig. 73).

In this Temperament we have long, massive bones; dense, tough, wiry muscles; steel-like tendons; and ligaments of iron—strength, endurance, capacity for physical exertion, both severe and prolonged; and, withal, a genuine love of work. It furnishes, then, considered in its mere bodily aspects, material for the rank and file of the great army of laborers— farmers, miners, lumbermen, artisans in all the heavier trades, sailors, soldiers, etc. Men of this constitution make the best pioneers of civilization in new countries. The forests fall before their strong arms. They patiently follow the plow which breaks up the broad prairie. The rough life of the new settler does not disgust or discourage them. No dangers can turn them from their course, and they fight Indians, contend against the elements and the beasts of the forest, or resist disease and death with the same unconquerable pluck and tenacity of purpose. They explore new regions; open new mines of gold, silver, or iron; build roads through the wilderness; and prepare the way for a higher civilization than they carry with them. Wherever there is hard work to be done, great obstacles to be overcome, imminent danger to be met, pluck, energy, and perseverance to be brought into action, we ought to find, and to a large extent do find, men of the Motive Temperament at the front.

As mechanics, men of the Motive Temperament should be iron-workers, stone-masons, blacksmiths, ship-builders, carpenters, etc.

But, so far, we have been considering this Temperament as exhibited on the lower plane of its activity—in persons in whom the mental system is not influential, or has not been awakened, drawn out, and developed by education and exercise. With a full (though subordinate) development of the mental system and a fair education, persons of the Motive Temperament become something more than mere hewers of wood and drawers of water. Workers they still necessarily are, but workers with the brain as well as with the hands, and the leaders and masters of others who work. They become navigators, discoverers, explorers, the founders of colonies, the builders and managers of railways, and the founders of great works generally—the master-spirits in all spheres of active life, where energy, courage, steadfastness, perseverance, and practical ability are most in demand. In times of political agitation, and in unsettled and lawless states of society, we often find them engaged in fomenting revolutions, heading insurrections, or leading unauthorized expeditions for the purpose of conquest or plunder. Restive under the restraints of even the most beneficent authority, loving liberty and hating tyranny in all its forms (except when exercised by themselves), they are ever ready to lead in " the fight for freedom ;" but so overmastering, in many cases, is their ambition and so insatiable their love of power, that they may, unless restrained by high moral principles, become worse tyrants than those they are so ready to overthrow.

It should be observed here that while the foregoing remarks apply in the main to persons of the

Motive Temperament generally, they are, in part, more emphatically true of those in whom the dark or bilious element is predominant, the sanguine variety showing somewhat less harshness and inflexibility, and not being so strongly disposed to domineer over all weaker natures.

It was fortunate for the American people that their Washington was a man of the Sanguine-Vital type (controlled by a predominant mental system) instead of the dark, bilious, or muscular constitution. The latter organization might have given them a more powerful leader, who would sooner and with more glory have driven the enemy from the soil, but it would probably also have given them a dictator and a dynasty instead of "the Father of his Country," who was not in love with power and who could lay down the reins with more pleasure than that which he felt in taking them up, at the call of his countrymen. By his side Cæsar and Napoleon are mere pretenders.

Though the Motive Temperament gives neither the taste nor any special fitness for either of the learned professions (so-called), yet where circumstances have led men of this constitution to become clergymen, lawyers, or physicians, they have sometimes, when well endowed intellectually, won distinction in their professions. Their proper place, however, is in the field rather than in the study, the office, or the court-room. As clergymen, they are adapted to missionary labors in heathen lands.

II.—ADAPTATIONS OF THE VITAL TEMPERAMENT
(Fig. 74).

What are the plump, round-faced, blue-eyed, ruddy, jovial, warm-hearted, good-natured subjects of the Vital Temperament best fitted for? They are full of life, zeal, enthusiasm, and impetuosity; love fresh air and outdoor exercise; have good, practical common sense, and a general. knowledge of men and things; are quick, shrewd, fertile in resources, versatile, and ready; but they lack depth of thought and accurate knowledge, steadiness, and perseverance; are impulsive and passionate; love pleasure more than duty, and are not fond of hard work.

Well, such persons can do many things, but prefer and are best fitted for the light, active employments which necessitate neither close confinement, continuous application, nor great muscular or mental exertion. Having generally large Acquisitiveness and a good, practical perceptive intellect, they do well in trade, with clerks to perform the drudgery and bear the confinement; they "know how to keep a hotel;" may become contractors, agents, and superintendents in various branches of business, or butchers, bakers, expressmen, and conductors, and are not averse to politics and public office.

With the Motive element of the constitution nearly equal, but subordinate to the Vital (as in Fig. 98), there will be immense capacity for steady, efficient effort, with a taste for hard work and close application; but the mental action will be slow and uncertain, and the character rather severe, harsh, and lacking in refinement.

FIG. 73.—ABRAHAM LINCOLN.

FIG. 74.—PERÉ HYACINTHE.

PLATE XXXIV.

The dark type, or Bilious-Vital Temperament, imparts more strength, perseverance, steadiness, and capacity for actual work, as also more pride, passion, and love of domination than the *xanthous* variety, or Sanguine-Vital.

Men of the Vital Temperament are to be found in all the professions, but they incline rather to medicine and divinity than to law, and with a good mental development often make very acceptable doctors and preachers. As physicians, their shrewdness, common sense, and intuitive knowledge of men, and, above all, their good-nature, sympathy, and cheerfulness, are often worth more to their patients than the accurate scientific attainments and profound professional learning, which they are pretty sure to lack, could possibly be. Their sunny disposition, their hopefulness, their strong vital magnetism, and their words of cheer, are better remedies than their drugs, and the sick ones to whom they are called begin to feel better before they have swallowed the first pill or globule.

As preachers, they are fluent, earnest, fervid, zealous, and impassioned, rather than scholarly, profound, argumentative, eloquent, or elevated in tone, appealing to the heart rather than to the head, and moving their hearers through the feelings rather than through the intellect.

III.—ADAPTATIONS OF THE MENTAL TEMPERAMENT (Fig. 75).

A comparatively slight and delicately organized body, small bones, thin muscles, slender limbs, and a relatively large and active brain, prominent characteristics of the Mental Temperament, suggest at once light employments, requiring intelligence and skill rather than muscular power. Small hands, a delicate touch, and keen eyesight fit persons of this Temperament for the lighter mechanical arts, like those of the watchmaker or jeweler, and for the construction of delicate machinery, mathematical instruments, etc.; also for the lighter branches of horticulture and trade.

But the literary and æsthetic tastes, characteristic of the mental organization, incline those in whom it is dominant to pursuits more purely intellectual or artistic—to divinity, medicine, law, journalism, authorship, teaching, painting, sculpture, music—in all of which the highest success may be attained, where the proper special mental developments exist, and there is sufficient vital stamina to sustain the necessary intellectual activity. In the tendency of this Temperament to mental application, and the neglect of physical exercise and recreation, lies its greatest danger. Its failures are generally due to physical weakness and to organic derangements acting upon the nervous system, rather than to a lack of the requisite cerebral development.

Compounding the Mental with a nearly equal proportion of the Bilious-Motive element in what we have called the Mental-Motive Temperament, we have the most powerful and effective organization conceivable for really great works of a solid, enduring, and useful nature, whether in literature, science, or the arts. It combines intellectual strength and

FIG. 75.—BISHOP J. T. LEWIS.

FIG. 76.—ANDREW JACKSON.

PLATE XXXV.

activity and moral elevation, with the cool, steady, persistent power of a dense and wiry physical organization, and is capable of that continuous and efficient effort in the chosen sphere of action which alone gives grand final results.

With the Vital next in strength and influence to the Mental element, there may be more brilliancy and a greater temporary success, but a less enduring fame, and a somewhat inferior capacity for usefulness in the spheres of practical life. This combination, however, gives us our greatest orators, our most elegant writers, as well as many great statesmen, divines, lawyers, and physicians.

IV.—SPECIAL DEVELOPMENT FOR PARTICULAR PURSUITS.

In addition to the temperamental qualifications suggested in the foregoing sections, each trade, profession, or occupation requires for its most efficient exercise certain special developments, as follows:

1. *The Law.*—Lawyers require large Eventuality, to recall lawcases and decisions; large Comparison, to compare different parts of the law and evidence—to criticise, cross-question, illustrate, and adduce similar cases; and large Language, to give freedom of speech.

2. *Statesmanship.*—Statesmen require large and well-balanced intellects, to enable them to understand and see through great public measures and choose the best course, together with high moral heads, to make them disinterested and seek the people's good, not selfish ends.

3. *Medicine.*—Physicians require large Perceptive Faculties, so that they may study and apply a knowledge of Anatomy and Physiology with skill and success; full Destructiveness, lest they shrink from inflicting the pain requisite to cure; large Constructiveness, to give them skill in surgery; large Combativeness, to render them resolute and prompt; large Cautiousness, to render them judicious and safe; and a large head, to give them general power of mind.

4. *Divinity.*—Clergymen require a large frontal and coronal region, the former to give them intellectual capacity, and the latter to impart high moral worth, aims, and feelings, elevation of character, and blamelessness of conduct; large Veneration, Hope, and Spirituality, to imbue them with the spirit of faith and devotion; large · Benevolence and Adhesiveness, so that they may make all who know them love them, and thus win each over to the paths of truth and righteousness. Clergymen will do well to consult Phrenology; it would enable them to account for many seeming mysteries, and give them power and influence to do great good. It is in the most perfect harmony with the highest Christianity.

5. *Journalism.*—Editors require large Individuality and Eventuality, to collect and disseminate incidents, facts, news, and give a practical cast of mind; large Comparison, to enable them to illustrate, criticise, show up errors, and the like; full or large Combativeness, to render them spirited; large Language, to render them copious, free, spicy, and racy; and large Ideality, to give taste and elevated sentiments. An editor who understands and applies Phrenology

possesses a power which he may use with great effect.

6. *Commerce.*—Merchants require Acquisitiveness, to impart a desire and tact for business; large Hope, to promote enterprise; full Cautiousness, to render them safe; large Perceptives, to give quick and correct judgment of the qualities of goods; good Calculation, to impart rapidity and correctness in casting accounts; large Approbativeness, to render them courteous and affable; and full Adhesiveness, to enable them to make friends of customers, and thus retain them. Why is one young man a better salesman than another? and why is one better worth a salary twice or thrice the amount than another? Phrenology answers this by pointing out the constitutional differences, and showing who is and who is not adapted to mercantile life.

7. *The Mechanic Arts.*—Mechanics require strong constitutions, to give them muscular power and love of labor; large Constructiveness and Imitation, to enable them to use tools with dexterity, work after a pattern, and easily do whatever they see others do; and large Perceptive Faculties, to give the required judgment of the qualities of materials and the fitness of things.

8. *The Fine Arts.*—Artists require high organic quality and large Ideality, to impart the necessary appreciation of the laws of beauty and the rules of taste; refinement, delicacy, imagination, and aspiration; Constructiveness, to give skill in the use of the implements of art; Imitation, to enable them to copy well; and large Perceptive Faculties, to impart judgment of the qualities and forms of objects.

XIII.

TEMPERAMENT IN HEALTH AND DISEASE.

IT is not our purpose to trench upon the domain of the medical writer, except so far as that domain is held in common by the physician and the physiologist—in other words, we shall call attention to the relations between Temperament and disease, not for the purpose of indicating what modifications of medical treatment the different constitutional conditions require, but in order, rather, to suggest the hygienic measures essential in each case to insure health of body and mental sanity. Incidentally, we have already touched upon this subject in previous chapters, and particularly in III. and IV., but it is too important in its bearings upon human welfare to be passed over without another and a more complete presenta tion, under its appropriate head.

I.—PREDISPOSITIONS OF THE MOTIVE TEMPERAMENT (Fig. 76).

The Motive Temperament gives great tenacity of life, and power to resist disease and its causes. It has, nevertheless, its weak points and its natural predispositions to certain forms of functional derangement, which those who possess it should know how to guard and counteract, so as to insure the health and longevity of which their constitution is susceptible.

(166)

In the first place, the hardiness, energy, and indifference to physical discomfort of persons of this Temperament lead to imprudent exposure to heat and cold, malaria, extreme fatigue, hurtful privations, and dietetic abuses, and thus render them liable to many diseases to which they are not, on constitutional grounds, particularly inclined. We can only warn such persons that even an iron constitution will finally give way before the assaults of diseases thus invited and fostered, and that neither honor nor profit are to be gained in the struggle against a fever or a pneumonia which might easily have been avoided.

The special predisposition of the Motive Temperament, especially in the dark variety, is to diseases of the stomach, more particularly those of a bilious character, and this predisposition is often strengthened by the conditions of climate, locality, diet, and mode of life under which this constitution finds its fullest development and its greatest activity. This tendency, being understood, may, in general, be readily counteracted by judicious hygienic measures.

1. In the first place, hot, malarious districts should, as far as possible, be avoided and the diet be chosen with reference to a cooling and diluent effect, to which end, salted and smoked meats, spices and condiments generally, tea, coffee, and spirituous liquors, should be avoided and their places supplied by fresh beef, mutton, poultry, and game, in moderate quantities, farinaceous foods, vegetables, and especially fruits.

2. The sanguine element of the Vital Tempera-

ment, being the natural antagonist of the bilious element of the Motive, should be zealously cultivated wherever there is a tendency to excessive or abnormal action of the latter, tending to functional derangement or disease. Some of the means of doing this consist in systematic exercises calculated to expand the lungs and aerate the blood, judicious bathing, recreation, and rest.

For the correction of the mental faults into which persons of this Temperament are prone to fall, partly through deranged bodily functions, such as violent outbursts of passion, offensive self-assertion, a domineering spirit, and a needlessly harsh exercise of legitimate authority, in addition to the hygienic measures suggested, there should be an assiduous cultivation of the mental constitution and especially of those sentiments which, like Benevolence, Approbativeness, and Agreeableness, tend to soften and humanize the character.

In health, the Motive Temperament, though it may not present, either in general contours or in particular features, forms equally agreeable to the eye of refined taste, as are seen in those of the other Temperaments, is not by any means deficient in attractions. It has a rough beauty, born of strength and firmness; a cool equipoise; and an air of simple dignity, such as self-reliance and consciousness of power always give, and commands respect if not admiration. Mentally, if it has not the genial good-nature of the Vital Temperament, or the refinement and delicate perceptions of what is fitting in manners and right morals that characterize the Mental Temperament; it is not, therefore, necessarily either rude, brusque, or otherwise offensive in social intercourse or regardless of the tastes, feelings, or rights of others. It is in its excessive development or its abnormal action that it becomes disagreeable and dangerous.

II.—PREDISPOSITIONS OF THE VITAL TEMPERAMENT (Fig. 77).

When we hear it remarked of a person that "he is the picture of health," we may safely infer, as a general rule, that the individual in question has the Vital Temperament. The full, round cheeks, the general plumpness, the fresh complexion, and the lively, cheerful expression of countenance which char-acterize this constitution, are popularly considered not merely as signs of health (which they certainly are in the case supposed), but as essential marks of bodily integrity and perfect functional action. The fact is, however, that the angular frame, prominent features, swarthy complexion, and severe gravity of countenance associated with the Motive Temperament, and the slight figure, sharp, delicate features, and earnest thoughtfulness, seen in the Mental Temperament, are equally consistent with perfect health ; and the practical lesson taught by these facts is that to judge correctly of a person's health, we must take into the account, as an important factor, his natural constitutional condition.

The Vital Temperament, undoubtedly, offers conditions exceedingly favorable to health and physical well-being. It necessarily involves, in full measure,

8

all the elements which are required to sustain in vigorous action both brain and muscle. There is good digestion, complete assimilation, strong circulation, and ample breathing power. Good blood in abundance is prepared, properly vitalized, propelled through every part of the system, and finally perfectly depurated, and its effete particles thrown out of the system by the proper outlets. The circle of animal life is unbroken. Added to this vital integrity, and partly dependent upon it, we find that amiable, joyous, hopeful, and contented disposition which is as favorable to bodily health as it is to happiness and peace of mind. But with all these advantages, this admirable constitution has its strong predispositions to derangement and disease. Complete fullness easily becomes overflowing excess, and here is just where the danger lies in this Temperament—in excess—in physical plethora and mental exuberance—whence come congestions, inflammations, intemperance, and sensuality.

The diseases to which the Vital Temperament is particularly predisposed, then, are those of a congestive and inflammatory character—fevers, rheumatism, apoplexy, acute disease of the heart, etc.—and to active hemorrhages ; and they are generally severe and rapid in their progress. The hygienic measures necessary to prevent the excessive development or abnormal activity of the nutritive system lie mainly in calling into more vigorous action the antagonistic forces of the locomotive and nervous systems, so as to decrease the relative influence of the vital element. To do this we must—

FIG. 77.—HON. HENRY WILSON.

FIG. 78.—MRS. MARIANNE WETMORE.

PLATE XXXVI.

1. Engage in some employment involving a large amount of active muscular exercise; or, this being impracticable, substitute systematic gymnastic exercises calculated to produce the same result—the increase of the locomotive system, and a corresponding relative decrease in the vital preponderance.

2. Cultivate the mental system by a close application to some business requiring the exercise of the intellectual powers; systematic study of some kind, particularly in the domain of science; reading, reflection, and intercourse with cultivated people—full activity for mind and body being the aim.

3. Regulate the diet so as to feed the muscular and nervous systems, rather than to stimulate the vital processes. For suggestions on the selection of foods for this purpose see Chapter IV., Section II.

As an auxiliary, the sedative action of water, judiciously applied, and of the Turkish bath, should be resorted to when practicable. Above all must the stimulation of high-seasoned foods, strong condiments, tea, coffee, and alcoholic liquors be avoided.

III.—PREDISPOSITIONS OF THE MENTAL TEMPERAMENT (Fig. 78).

Persons in whom the Mental Temperament is strongly developed are frequently more thin and pale than is consistent with our notions of perfect health; but these individuals, other things being equal, are less frequently ill, and are longer-lived than the plump, ruddy, full-blooded subjects of the Vital Temperament; from which fact, however, the true inference is not that emaciation and pallor are

signs of a better physical condition than that indicated by the opposite qualities in contour and color,
but that they are not, in persons of the Mental Temperament, symptoms of absolute ill-health.   They
are simply indicative of a too great activity of the
brain relatively to the vigor of the vital system—a
condition by no means desirable, but, at the same
time, less rather than more subversive of health than
excessive vital action.   A balance between these
forces constitutes the golden mean of the highest
health and the greatest mental power.   .

The diseases to which persons of the Mental Temperament are predisposed are those of a nervous and
spasmodic character, manifesting themselves in many
forms, but especially in headache, neuralgia, sleep-
lessness, indigestion, palpitations of the heart, and
tremors.   Insanity and other mental affections are
also among the dangers to which excessive mental
action, not sufficiently sustained by vital stamina,
may lead.

- As these ailments are mainly due to physical weakness, consequent upon the undue exhaustion of the
vital powers through a too great activity of the
brain, the obvious remedial and preventive measures
must lie in restoring the balance between supply and
demand in these particulars.   There must be—

1. A decrease of expenditure in the vital economy,
to be effected by allowing the mind more rest and
recreation—by running the mental machinery more
slowly, and fewer hours per day.

2. An increase of the vital element through a nutritious diet, rest, sleep, and recreation.   The dis-

position to neglect the wants of the body, while ministering to the demands of the mental appetite; the constant application to study, the subjection of the whole being to overmastering thought, must be overcome, and a regimen adopted which shall give the nutritive system its proper influence in the organization. Tea, coffee, tobacco, late hours, and all 'cinds of dissipation must be entirely avoided. The diet should not only be nutritious, but easy of digestion, and the exercise taken must be suited to the strength, and of a character to divert the mind while strengthening the body. In a word, the vital or nutritive system must be cultivated, and the mental system be restrained.

IV.—General Hygienic Considerations.

There are certain general hygienic considerations which will apply, in the main, to all varieties of constitution, and may appropriately be added here to the brief hints given for each specifically. Health is the natural condition in each Temperament, and disease the abnormal state; so that we have but to follow Nature's laws in each case to attain and retain physical integrity and functional harmony.

Health depends upon the existence of certain conditions clearly indicated in our physical and mental constitution, such as—

1. A sound physical organization;
2. A vigorous, well-balanced mind;
3. A constant and adequate supply, and the right use of all the elements essential to the sustenance of the body.

If the first two of these conditions are not ours by inheritance, we can only measurably supply the lack by judicious cultivation, the means for doing which are detailed in works devoted to physiology, hygiene, gymnastics, and mental science. Coming, then, to the third specification, we may particularize as elements essential to the sustenance and health of the body—air, sunlight, food, drink, physical exercise, rest, sleep, cleanliness, mental activity, and harmonious social relations.

(1). Air is the first and last demand of our lives. We must have it, sleeping or waking, every day and hour from birth to death; and to be healthy we must have pure air. Out of doors we can generally get this, but in close rooms the case is entirely different. "A single person will deprive from one to two hogsheads of air of its blood-purifying qualities, and saturate it with poisonous gases in a single hour. In the light of this fact, consider what must be the effects of the in-door life of our people, and especially of our women. Think of our crowded work-rooms; of family gatherings around the sitting-room stove; of evening parties in unventilated parlors, where the lights which make everything so brilliant rapidly hasten the deteriorating process which respiration has commenced; and of two or more persons sleeping all night in a close seven-by-nine bedroom. 'Close bedrooms,' Dr. Hall says, 'make the graves of thousands.' The occasional opening of doors gives us now and then a breath of fresh air in the rooms occupied during the day; but even this is denied us in our sleeping apartments." Everything, then, which vitiates the air should carefully be excluded from our rooms, and especially our bedrooms, and the outdoor air admitted as freely as circumstances will admit ; and we should spend as much of our time out of doors as possible, taking exercise calculated to expand the lungs and maintain (and increase, if necessary) our breathing power.

(2). Solar light, although generally left almost entirely out of the account by many physiological and hygienic writers, has a great and striking effect upon the human physical system. Without it, in fact, nothing like perfect bodily development, health, or beauty can possibly exist. It is well known that plants growing in the shade or in darkness are always slender, weak, and pale. Deprivation of light has a similar effect upon man, as shown by persons confined in dungeons, mines, and dark habitations. Women who avoid the sunlight and darken their parlors and sitting-rooms, through fear of spoiling their complexions, invite thereby the very evil they desire to avoid.

(3). The subject of food is perhaps the most important one in the whole range of hygienic inquiry, and much too extensive for proper treatment here. All we can hope to do is to give a few hints which will at least put the reader in the way to look into the matter further for himself.

A writer whom we find quoted in a work on phys· ical culture, now before us, and who has given some excellent hints toward a system of dietetics founded on the firm basis of science, lays down the broad principle that " the body itself is the rule of its food—

that is, as is the chemical nature of the body at large, such must be the chemical nature of the entire mass of aliments taken; and as is the nature of each particular structure to which we would secure nutriment and efficiency, such must be the nature of the particular aliment employed to that end; but this law is modified by another equally imperative one, namely: that *exercise is the rule of food*—that is, the food we eat should contain as nearly as possible the several elements in the same proportion as their expenditure occurs in the individual system of the consumer, owing to his particular mental and physical activities." In other words, if a man exercise his muscles largely, he should consume largely of muscle-forming aliment; and if he work his brain continually, he must satisfy the cravings of the system with brain-food.

(*a*). The plastic, cell-forming, or nutritive aliments are albumen and the substances usually grouped with it—gluten, casein, and the substance of muscle-fiber, nerve-tube, and cell-membrane; the calorific or respiratory foods are sugar, starch, and the oils or fats; the acids are cooling, purifying, and blood-perfecting in their action; water is indispensable, both as vehicle and material to digestion, absorption, assimilation, circulation, nutrition, secretion, and excretion, muscular and brain-action; the inorganic elements other than water, sometimes called nutritive minerals, have various uses.

(*b*). Among the alimentary compounds particularly fitted to produce muscle are wheat-meal, corn-meal, beans, cabbages, carrots, and the flesh of quadrupeds while eggs, nuts, cream (milk), fish, and the flesh of poultry are specially adapted to nourish the brain. "Oatmeal and milk seem to belong to both classes of aliments; and rice, potatoes, fruits, and a large list of foods may be styled indifferent, as specially favoring neither development.

(*c*). "The diet of no two persons should be, in reality, exactly alike, since their constitutions, states of health, avocations, and forms and amounts of physical expenditure are necessarily different.

(*d*). "Insufficient variety in food is as great an evil as insufficiency in the quantity of food, and an evil of the same kind; because it necessarily withholds from the system a due supply of some one or more essential forms of aliment. A moderate variety is desirable at every meal; a greater, from day to day.

(*e*). "That diet is most perfect for each individual which furnishes to each the various forms of substance necessary to make up his fluids and solid tissues, and in the same proportion as they exist and are daily expended in his particular constitution and mode of life.

(*f*). "Muscle and nerve both necessitate albuminous food; the former, in connection with the finer or phosphorized fatty substances; the latter, with the grosser fats and the phosphate and carbonate of lime.

(*g*). "Excess in food is not to be defined by any particular quantity. It exists only when there is a surplus over healthful expenditure; and by this rule one adult system may require more than twice the amount of food demanded by another.

8*

(*h*). " Both vegetable and animal foods have their uses ; the former favor and support more especially the organic development and processes, such as nutrition and secretion ; the latter, the animal or active functions, such as locomotion, will-power, and intellectual action.

(*i*). " No imperfect vegetable or animal production, as those that are dwarfed, or sickly, or immature, or undergoing decay, can furnish materials for complete human alimentation.

(*j*). " Some foods constitute necessary compensating adjuncts to others and should be used with them. Thus rice, corn, or potatoes require the addition of wheat-meal bread, or flesh, or milk and eggs, to supply the albuminous and mineral elements which they possess in a less degree. So beans, peas, cabbage, cauliflower, asparagus, etc., lack the oleaginous element and this should be added in the cooking.

(*k*). " A larger proportion of fatty or heat-producing food is required in winter than in summer, and in northern than in southern climates."

(4). For a universal drink, we can safely recommend water; and we suppose there will be few to call our recommendation in question, though there have been theorists who have contended that man is not naturally a drinking animal.

(5). In connection with what is received into the system, in the form of food and drink, the excretions, or what passes off by the natural outlets of the body, should be considered. These are the worn-out materials of the system, and those parts of the food which, although perhaps of the greatest use, are not .

assimilable. Retained in the system, they poison its fluids and ultimately destroy its tissues. The complete and regular performance of the excretory functions is therefore of the utmost importance. A stoppage of the bowels or of the pores of the skin can not exist for a single day without positive injury to the health. A too great relaxation, on the other hand, is equally to be avoided.

A properly regulated diet will generally insure regularity and efficiency in the action of the bowels. Among the foods of a constipating tendency are bread and cakes from fine wheaten flour, rice, beans, flesh meats, eggs, and tea. Bread from wheaten meal or unbolted flour, rye, or corn; fruits, raw and cooked; and generally substances abounding in ligneous matter, are laxative in their tendency.

Should costiveness or diarrhœa occur, the cause should be ascertained at once and removed. This will generally suffice to restore healthy action; if not, resort to injections of pure water, which seldom or never fail, avoiding purgative medicines, which have a tendency to increase, in the end, the very difficulty they are intended to remedy.

(6). The necessity of bodily exercise has been insisted upon in previous chapters. The amount required varies with age, sex, and Temperament; but no person can enjoy vigorous health, or acquire or retain any high degree of personal beauty, without more or less active bodily exertion. The women of our country are suffering incalculably for want of the proper exercise of their muscles. Exercise in the open air should be an every-day duty and an every-day pleasure, with every man, woman, and child.

(7). If exercise is essential to human well-being, repose is not less so. The one is the complement of the other. Without exercise, repose would have no meaning and no use; and without repose, exercise would soon wear out and destroy the body. Nothing can be more essential to continued health and physical well-being than regular habits in regard to sleep. The amount required varies with different persons and circumstances, but there must be no attempt to cheat Nature, by allowing too little.

(8). "Dirt upon the skin," Wilkinson says, "is not merely dirt, but dirty feeling; and the latter is no sooner set up than it travels soulward;" while cleanliness "places a cordon of pure life around our bodies, as a troop of angels around the bed, and before the path of the faithful." If one would be healthy he must keep the millions of pores which permeate the skin constantly open, which means that he must keep clean. As a general rule, the whole body should be washed all over every day in summer, and at least once a week in winter. Tepid water—say from 80° to 92°—or that which feels slightly cool, but not cold to the body, is best for general use. The cold bath is a powerful stimulus, and, like other stimuli, must be used in moderation and with good judgment. The skin as well as the stomach may be stimulated too much.

(9). Mental activity has already been shown to be almost as essential to health as bodily exercise; but to act is not enough. We must also enjoy. "Sorrow," Melancthon says, "strikes the heart, and makes it flutter and pine away with great pain." And if one merely feels "stupid," or is "out of humor," or has the "blues," he is already half sick, and likely soon to be wholly so. The cheerful man digests his food properly; his blood circulates freely, and his system is duly nourished; but depress his mind with sorrow or care, and all his functions are obstructed and he grows lean and pale.

(10). Finally, the affections must also find their satisfaction in our lives. Unsatisfied longing for love, for the joys of maternity, or for the companionship of kindred and friends, depress the vital energies, wither the roses and lilies of the cheek, and dim the light of the eye. Unhappy marriages, and family discords in general, bring with them physical derangement as well as mental suffering. The whole man must be in harmony with itself and with all surrounding circumstances, or perfect health can not be enjoyed.*

---

* Hints Toward Physical Perfection.

XIV.

TEMPERAMENT IN RACES AND NATIONS.

TEMPERAMENT has been studied and written upon mainly with reference to the Caucasian race, and to that race alone will our remarks in the preceding pages apply in full, though the general principles on which all temperamental distinctions are based are, of course, universal. The same anatomical structure, in its general features at least, is common to all races. The bony framework with its ligaments, muscles, and tendons, furnishes in all the basis for a Motive Temperament; the nutritive apparatus, with its wonderfully constructed organs of digestion, secretion, and circulation, everywhere gives us the vital element of the constitution; and in no tribe of men, however low in the scale of intelligence, is the brain and nervous system wholly lacking; but when we come to the details of configuration, complexion, texture, and functional action, we find our descriptions, made for the white races, are applicable only in part to the others. A Negro may have the Vital Temperament, even in its sanguine form, but the florid complexion, light hair, blue eyes, and some other characteristics of that constitution, as found in the Caucasian, are lacking; so the American Indian is copper-colored and the Mongolian tawny, whether their Temperament be Bilious or not. It is plain, then, that our descriptions must be remodeled to adapt them to the dark races.

We approach this part of our subject with diffi-dence, confessing, in the outset, that our knowledge of the constitutional characteristics of some of the races and sub-races, into which the genus *homo* has been divided, are merely general, and imperfect at that, so as to preclude the close analysis we have applied to the organization of our own race. We offer the following remarks, therefore, so far as they relate to the dark races particularly, rather as hints toward a correct temperamental description, than as statements of facts, in all cases absolutely demonstrated. If not always correct in our conclusions, we trust that even our errors will lead, through the investigation they may incite, to the final establishment of the truth.

I.—THE RACES CLASSIFIED.

There are numerous classifications of the human races, each writer on ethnology apparently invent-ing one to suit his peculiar theory or method of treat-ment. We can not here stop to discuss either the theories or the nomenclature of these writers, but shall adopt, as well enough suited to our purpose, and more generally known than most others, the class-ification of Blumenbach, in which are recognized five races, as follows:

1. The Caucasian Race
2. The Mongolian Race;
3. The Malayan Race;
4. The American Race; and
5. The Ethiopian Race.

Of these five races, or groups of races, if the readei choose so to consider them, we now propose to take a general view from the stand-point of temperamental physiology.

II.—TEMPERAMENT IN THE CAUCASIAN RACE.

In this branch of the human family, as we have seen in the preceding chapters, all the Temperaments are fully represented—the Sanguine, the Bilious, the Lymphatic, the Nervous; or the Vital, the Motive, and the Mental—and all have well-understood characteristics and modes of manifestation. The tendency among the more advanced nations, families, and individuals of the race, however, is evidently toward a preponderance of the Mental system—in other words, the Mental Temperament is its typical constitutional condition; and this seems to have been the case from the earliest periods of which history or tradition gives any account.

1. *The Ancient Greeks.*—The Mental Temperament is evident enough in the works as well as in the portraits of the Hellenic peoples, notwithstanding the prominence given to bone and muscle in their sedulous culture of the physical system. Their supremacy in the arts and in literature was due to the fine-grained, complexly convoluted, and massive brains, which filled and molded their smooth, round, symmetrical craniums. A high quality of organization, and a clear, sharp, active intellect, strong alike in perception and in reflection, made the Greek what he was as artist, poet, orator, and philosopher. The Mental Temperament in him seems to have lacked,

however, in some degree, the high coronal development generally associated with it in more modern times.
His strong impulses were but imperfectly controlled
by moral sentiment, and his intellectual gifts seldom
sanctified by any lofty spiritual purpose.

2. *The Ancient Roman* (Fig. 79).—The Roman cranium was as unlike the Greek as the art, literature,
and history of Rome is unlike that of Greece. It was
equally massive, but less symmetrical, coarser-grained,
and more angular. It showed, as the apex of its development, very large Firmness, the lines sloping from
that point ; the forehead was massive, but broad rather
than high; the Perceptive Faculties were well-developed and vigorous, especially those giving accurate
observation and practical ability; the reasoning powers
were good ; and the moral sentiments very unevenly
developed, Conscientiousness largely predominating
over Benevolence, and Self-esteem over Spirituality.
The head had great lateral expansion at the base,
giving ample room for the propelling or executive
organs.

With such a head the Temperament of the ancient
Roman, it will be seen, must necessarily have had a
strong physical basis in the locomotive system. That
this was the fact, Roman history completely demon-
strates. The Roman Temperament was the Motive
or Bilious (or more definitely, Bilious-Motive), the
Mental, of course, gaining the ascendency in numerous
cases among the leading men of the higher classes,
but being always invigorated, intensified, and made
terribly effective by the dense underlying stratum of
the bilious-muscular constitution ; and this organiza-

tion furnishes the key to Roman character and history. A late ethnological writer, speaking of the
cause of Roman supremacy, says :

" The Roman organization, like the Roman mind,
was powerful rather than harmonious, and more distinguished by vigor than refinement. . . . . The
Temperament was intensely fibrous, and must have
effectually re-invigorated the tendencies arising from
organization. Indeed, the stern endurance, unswerv-
ing fixity of purpose, and dauntless moral courage of
the ancient Roman were due almost as much to the
former as the latter. He was a man of iron mold,
both in body and mind, and in the path of duty unsus-
ceptible of the softer emotions and 'inaccessible to
the gentler feelings. Patriotism was his master passion, and obedience to the law his highest virtue. He
preferred precedent to principle, and was governed
by authority rather than reason. And how accurately
is all this mirrored in those high, proud, angular features, constituting that stern, expressive, and commanding countenance ! And how forcibly is it indicated to the ethnological and physiological eye, in
that compact and muscular frame, with the broad and
powerful chest, surmounted by a head and neck so
eminently indicative of energy and self-reliance—of
the power that marches slowly, but invincibly, to its
purpose, that accomplishes its most important objects
with the greatest deliberation, and is not in haste even
for the conquest of a world ! "

Our likeness of Julius Cæsar (Fig. 79), from a copy
of a very ancient drawing, while showing a large head
and an undoubted predominance of the Mental sys-

tem, shows with equal plainness the indications of the tough, hard, fibrous physical constitution on which his intellectual power rested—in other words, it represents the Mental-Motive Temperament.

3. *The Semite or Syro-Arabian.*—The Semitic sub-race comprises the Arabians, the Assyrians, the Chaldeans, the Hebrews, and cognate tribes, among whom the same form of skull prevails, and whose temperamental characteristics are similar.

The head in these tribes is smaller than in the European nations, and less developed in the region of the Reflective Faculties, giving the forehead a retreating aspect; but it is remarkable for its grandly elevated coronal arch, indicating great development in the central line of the top-head. The base of the brain is rather broad, being particularly full in the region of Acquisitiveness; but the dominating influence lies in the spiritual part of the brain; and the Semite, whether Arab, Syrian, or Jew, is essentially a religious enthusiast—as some one has aptly said: "His first and strongest impulse is to worship and propagate his faith; the second, to *trade.*"

In Temperament there is considerable variety, but in nearly all cases there is a strong development of the Bilious element, associated often, especially among the Jews, with a predominance of the Vital instead of the Motive constitution (the Bilious-Vital Temperament). The Mental element is always influential, especially in its intuitive manifestations.

"Arabs in the desert, Chaldeans on the Euphrates, Syrians at Damascus, Phœnicians at Tyre, Israelites at Jerusalem, Saracens at Bagdad, and, we may add,

Moors at Cordova, the Semitic tribes, though wild and unsubduable by the softening influences of civilization in the remoter fastnesses of their native habitat, have, nevertheless, shown considerable aptitude both for literature and science, when subjected to culture at the great urban centers of intellectual activity and refinement. Everywhere merchants, and always religious enthusiasts, they have also occasionally approved themselves as scholars and philosophers, physical and metaphysical, of no mean order. More robust, but less subtile in their mental constitution than the Hindoos—more prone to emo ion and less qualified for speculation—active, enterprising, energetic, chivalrous, and devout, they furnish a providential link between the dreamily meditative theosophy of the farther East, and the almost rude practicality of the extreme West."

4. *The Hindoo* (Fig. 80). — The true high-caste Hindoo has a comparatively small, but symmetrically formed cranium of a fine texture, a delicate and refined physical organization, well-chiseled features, and a gentle, reflective, reverential aspect. His Temperament is decidedly Mental.

The Hindoo head is high, but narrow at the base, indicating the predominance of the moral and imaginative elements over the propensities, and a lack of courage and force of character. Veneration is strongly developed and active; hence his whole life is a series of religious acts, and persons and places, as well as the gods themselves, are objects of his reverence. He is the product of a long-existent, but decadent civilization, and bears the marks of its

FIG. 79.—THE ANCIENT ROMAN. JULIUS CÆSAR.

FIG. 80.—HIGH CASTE HINDOO.

PLATE XXXVII.

culture, but suffers from the decrepitude consequent upon its exhaustion.

Such men as the fierce Nena Sahib, nominally Hindoos, have other blood in their veins, and broader bases to their skulls.

5. *The German* (Fig. 81).—The German of the present day is the best representative we have of the Teutonic branch of the great Caucasian race, which embraces also the Norwegian, the Swede, the Dane, the Anglo-Saxon, and the Anglo-American.

The Temperament of the German has always for the physical basis of its powerful mentality a strong substratum of the Sanguine-Vital element, with a sufficient development of the Motive or muscular constitution to give firmness, stability, and persistence to the character—in other words, there is a good balance of organization.

Professor Morton found the mean internal capacity of fifteen German skulls, measured by him, to be ninety-five cubic inches. The regions of the Reflective Faculties and of the Moral Sentiments are particularly well marked; the Perceptive Faculties, except Time and Tune, are less prominent. Ideality, Constructiveness, Alimentiveness, Acquisitiveness, Secretiveness, and Self-esteem are generally conspicuously large.

The German is, by nature, an inventor, an investigator, an experimenter, a thinker. Slow, but industrious, patient, and persevering; no mental task is too formidable for him to undertake; no problem so profound that he dare not seek to solve it; but while he discovers many new truths, he often leaves it for others to make a practical application of them.

6. *The Scandinavian* (Fig. 82).—The Danes, Swedes and Norwegians comprise the principal branches of the Scandinavian family, which seems to form the culminating point of the old Gothic race—the tall, muscular, blue-eyed, fair-haired people of Northern and Western Europe. Each has its national peculiarities, but all bear a strong family resemblance.

The Scandinavian, and notably the Norwegian, furnishes an admirable illustration of what we have elsewhere (Chapters IV. and VI.) described as the *xanthous* or Sanguine variety of the Motive Temperament, in which the blue eyes, light hair, and florid complexion which we are accustomed to associate with the Vital Temperament, and which certainly indicate the sanguine element, strongly developed, are conjoined with the large bones, strong articulations, dense, wiry muscles, angular configuration, and prominent features, which characterize the muscular or Motive constitution. The mental characteristics are those of the Motive Temperament, somewhat modified by the more impressible and flexible sanguine element infused.

Compared with the German, the Scandinavian is more active in body and mind, and more practical in his tendencies. "His frame is larger and taller, his muscles more dense, his features more prominent, his perceptive faculties more fully developed, and his Causality less prominent, though by no means deficient. He has quite as high a top-head as the German, and his grand mythology indicates the mystic sublimity of his ideas; and with all his practicality he has given us Swedenborg, the greatest and purest

FIG. 81.—THE GERMAN. JOSEPH FRANCOIS GALL, M.D.

FIG. 82.—THE SCANDINAVIAN. JOHN ERICSSON.

PLATE XXXVIII

as well as the most learned and scientific of all the mystics. In war, Scandinavia boasts her Charles XII.; in natural science, her Linnæus; in song, her Jenny Lind; and in literature, her Frederica Bremer. To us she has given her Ericsson, with his caloric engine and his *Monitor*, who may fitly represent the practical phase of Scandinavian character."

7. *The Englishman* (Fig. 83).—The Anglo-Saxon of England is a modified Teuton, the product of a very complete amalgamation of several ethnic elements, among which the Gothic predominates. His cranium is large; well-developed in the region of the reflective faculties; broad over the ear (Executiveness); prominent at Cautiousness and Self-esteem, and not lacking in the perceptive organs. The Temperament, whatever may be superinduced, has always an ample physical basis in a well-developed vital system—in fact, the Vital Temperament is the national one, the exceptions being a Mental predominance, the result of high culture and the external conditions of advanced civilization, or a Lymphatic degeneration, caused by a moist climate and bodily habits unfavorable to health.

Mentally, the Englishman is ambitious, energetic, aggressive, acquisitive, combative, proud, self-sufficient, domineering, firm, cautious, affectionate, and benevolent. His heart is warm and his feelings tender, though his manners and speech may at times be rough. He is more noted for common sense than for metaphysical acuteness, imagination, or sentimentality.

8. *The Anglo-American* (Fig. 84).—Americans of

the United States have hardly had time to develop
a national type of cranium or a national Temperament.   The basis on which we are to raise the
superstructure of a distinctive national organization
and character, however, is Anglo-Saxon, or English.
Climate and other external conditions, together with
the admixture of Celtic blood, have already greatly
modified our skulls, our physiognomy, and our Temperament.   If not distinctively national in constitution, we certainly are not English.   Our heads are
longer, our facial bones narrower, our features more
prominent, our muscles more dense and wiry.   The
Englishman is sanguine, the American nervous-bil-
ious; the vital or nutritive system predominates in
the former, the locomotive (muscular and osseous) in
the latter.   The English have more Self-esteem than
Approbativeness; with us it is the reverse.   They
have more Veneration, we more Benevolence.   We
are more active, intuitive, and generous; the English
more considerate, prudent, and reserved.

What the American of the future shall be, those
who live generations hence will know.   We can only
conjecture that the modifications now observable, as
gradually going on in our physical and mental organization, will be carried still further, and that the final
result will be that perfect adaptation in physical
constitution, conformation, complexion, and mental
character to the American climate, which will insure
the highest health and the greatest longevity, as well
as a fixed national or American type.

9. *The Scotchman.*—The Scotsman of the Low-
lands is of a mixed Celto-Saxon lineage, and his

FIG. 83.—JOHN BRIGHT.

ENGLISHMAN.

PLATE XXXIx

cranium, configuration of body, cast of features, Temperament, and character differ widely from those of his English neighbors. His head is longer than the English type, and proportionally narrower anteriorly. It is full, however, at the base, in the region of Cautiousness, Combativeness, Acquisitiveness, and Secretiveness. The Moral Sentiments generally are well-developed, as are Causality, Comparison, and the Perceptive Faculties. Ideality and Imitation are deficient. The Temperament is Motive, with the Sanguine infusion, as in the case of the Scandinavian, or in the educated classes Mental-Motive ; the complexion being light, the eyes blue or gray, and the hair light-brown, sandy, or red. The stature is generally above the medium, the frame strong and sinewy, and the features rather prominent, but sharply cut.

As a result of this organization, the Lowland Scot is profoundly discriminating in abstract philosophical inquiries, accurate in practical science, a close observer, shrewd in business, cautious, secretive, economical, persevering, set in his way, quick to resist, fond of controversy, religious, and steadfast. He lacks imagination, and has little taste for poetry and the fine arts.

The Highlanders of the better class are Gothic in their characteristics, resembling the Norwegians, from whom they are descended, in Temperament and configuration, while the common people are mainly Celtic, and have the Motive Temperament of the dark or bilious type.

Unlike the Lowlander, the Highland Scot of the higher class is ardent, impulsive, sensitive, urbane,

9

generous, open, vivacious, passionate, and imaginative.

10. *The Irishman.*—In the northern part of Ireland many of the people closely resemble those of Scotland, and are doubtless of Gothic origin, but the nation is, in the main, Celtic, and has the combination of temperamental elements, found occasionally in all Caucasian races, in which a strong infusion of the bilious element co-exists with a predominance of the Vital system, and many peculiarities of the Sanguine constitution. The typical Irishman is well-made, broad-chested, and strong-limbed ; less rounded in his contours than the Englishman, but more tense, wiry, and tough. His features are rather strongly marked and prominent, his hair dark, and his eyes black, brown, or gray. He is impulsive, enthusiastic, ardent, social, sympathetic, full of feeling, kind-hearted, lively, and witty. He is a natural orator, and excels in lyric poetry. He is intensely patriotic, full of schemes for the deliverance of his country, but wanting in wise forethought, caution, and practical common sense. Fond of jovial companionship and stimulating beverages, he is liable to be led by his appetites into various excesses, ruinous alike to body and mind.

11. *The Frenchman* (Fig. 85).—The French head, which may be considered as best representing the civilized Celt of the present day, is thus described by Dr. Vimont, himself a Frenchman :

" The French head is smaller than the German. The region of the perceptive faculties, as a whole, is larger and that of the reflectives smaller in the French

FIG. 84.—THE AMERICAN. SAMUEL R. WELLS.

PLATE XL.

than in the German head. The organs of Time, Tune, and Number, however, are larger in the German head. The French are generally deficient in the organ of Cautiousness. Individuality and Form are generally large, as are also those of Comparison, Wit, Wonder, Sublimity, and Poetry [*Talent Poetique*, according to Gall, whom Vimont here follows]. Constructiveness, Imitation, and Sense of the Beautiful [Ideality] are large, especially the last two. Love of Approbation is generally predominant, while Self-esteem and Firmness are moderate or small. Veneration is deficient, but Benevolence is well developed."

He might have added that Amativeness, Combativeness, Secretiveness, and Language are generally particularly well developed, and that the Moral Sentiments as a group are rather deficient, and have too little influence on the French character.

In Temperament, the Frenchman, like all other true Celts, has the bilious element as the basis, but in the cultivated classes the mental system predominates, with an infusion of the sanguine sufficient to give vivacity, versatility, brilliant cleverness, and love of novelty and change. He displays all the energy and directness of the Motive Temperament, but fails to illustrate its steadfastness and persistence. He is tasteful in dress; a model of politeness; lively and witty in conversation; a good actor, and a dashing, fearless soldier. In intellect he is clear, acute, vigorous, and discriminating, but not profound; subtle, ingenious, and penetrating, but not so original or inventive; socially, he is friendly and loving, but often inconstant in his affections. As a writer, he is animated, facile, dramatic; rich in all the ornaments of style, in verbal niceties and in apt illustrations, but often verbose and tedious.

12. *The Italian* (Fig. 86).—The great diversity of race in Italy renders it impossible to give any description which will apply to the nation as a whole. Gothic in Lombardy, Piedmont, Parma, Modena, Bologna, and Romagna; Etruscan in Tuscany; Liguorian in Genoa; Greek in Naples; semi-Moorish in Sicily and Sardinia, where shall we find the typical Italian? We may say in general terms, that the higher classes of Italy furnish us with some of the finest examples of the Mental Temperament to be found anywhere. Inheriting the results of many centuries of civilization, they have all the delicacy and refinement that a fine-grained physical organization can give, and all the artistic taste and love of beauty which comes through generations of culture; and these classes have given us the great men who have made Italy illustrious— Michael Angelo, Raphael, Dante, Petrarch, Tasso, Galileo, Columbus, Cavour, and Mazzini—to say nothing of Napoleon, a Corsican by birth, an Italian by descent, and Greco-Roman by blood.

13. *The Spaniard* (Fig. 87). — The Spaniard—a Celt-Iberian, with infusions of Phœnician, Greek, Roman, Gothic, Jewish, and Moorish blood — is moderate in stature, rather stout, well-formed, firm-fleshed, compact, muscular, and hardy, with a cranium broader than that of the Frenchman, and higher in the crown; a rounder face, less prominent features, a swarthy complexion, black hair, and black or brown eyes, indicating what may be called, under

FIG. 85.—THE FRENCHMAN. JEAN L. E. MESSONIER.

FIG. 86.—THE ITALIAN. MAZZINI.

PLATE XLI.

the old classification, the Sanguine-Bilious Temperament; or, as we have suggested elsewhere, the Bilious-Vital — the bilious element being very influential, and showing itself very prominently in the character, which is firm, self-reliant, proud, grave, courteous, affable, brave, devotional, passionate, secretive, politic, persistent, fanatical, cruel, revengeful, and relentless.*

14. *The Sclavon* (Fig. 88).—It is estimated that nearly *eighty millions* of human beings are linked together under this racial name, and throughout the whole mass there is a strong sentiment of race and a disposition among all the tribes into which it is divided to make a common cause with each other against any foe from without.

We will take the Russian proper—the Muscovite— as a type of the Sclavonic race, and as probably the future master of the destinies of Europe.

The Temperament of the Russian is Vital, or in the higher classes, Mental-Vital, with the muscular or Motive element sufficiently influential to give great toughness and endurance to the physical system and remarkable steadiness, self-poise, and persistence to the mental character. His most striking physical characteristic is *breadth*. He is broadheaded, broad-shouldered, broad-chested, thick-set, short-limbed, and muscular, and his respiration, cir-

---

* De La Sarthe, speaking of the Temperament of the Spaniard, says : " *Constitution bileuse ; démarche arrogant ; physiognomie vaniteuse et suffisante ; esprit cauteleux, difficile ; caractere orgueilleux et vindictif.*"

culation, and digestion are all equally good. The
complexion of the true Russian is light, and his eyes
blue, but in the South, a mixture of Servian blood,
climatic influences, etc., give him a darker hue.

Mentally the Russian has all the solidity, soundness, comprehensiveness, and vigor which his organization would lead us to expect. " The heavy basilar
region betokens the immense animal power and executiveness which underlie an intellect of no mean
order, and, in the higher classes, a full development
of the moral sentiments. He has not yet developed
any great originality, but he is an apt scholar, and
not ashamed to take lessons even of his enemies.
He will yet *teach* in his turn. He is naturally inclined to peace, and to the peaceful pursuit of agriculture; but when called upon to do it, fights with
cool courage and unconquerable persistence."

The Poles form another branch of the Sclavonic
race, and to the same general characteristics as are
shown by the Russians, add greater activity, ardor,
and impulsiveness, with some of the refining influences of a more ancient civilization. Many of
them have dark hair and eyes, and are taller and
more elegantly formed than the Sclavons generally.
Their strong national feeling does not readily allow
itself to be absorbed in the racial spirit.

III.—TEMPERAMENT IN THE MONGOLIAN RACE.

This race embraces the nations and tribes which
occupy the central, eastern, south-eastern, and northern parts of Asia—the people of China, Japan, Thibet,
Bootan, and Indo-China, the Laplanders of Europe,

FIG. 87.—THE SPANIARD. CORTEZ.

FIG. 88.—THE SCLAVAN. ALEXANDER ALEXANDROVITCH.

PLATE XLII

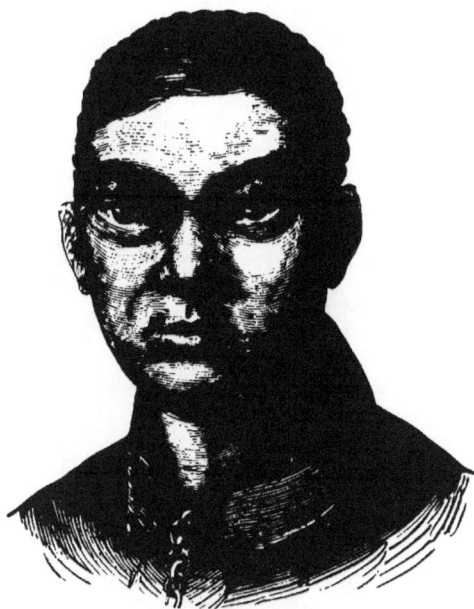

FIG. 89.—A CHINAMAN.

FIG. 90.—A MALAY.

PLATE XLIII.

and the Esquimaux, on the shores of the Arctic Ocean. A portion of the race, notably the Chinese and Japanese, are the depositories of an old, and, in some respects, a high civilization, but one seemingly incapable of much advancement.

Taking the Chinese (Fig. 89) as a type of the Mongolian race, we find the prevailing Temperament to be Bilious-Vital, with a strong predisposition to the Lymphatic condition, especially among those residing in moist or marshy regions. The Mental Temperament is not unknown among the Chinese and Japanese, but is far from being common.

The Mongolian head is smaller than that of the Caucasian, and has a larger proportion of its bulk back of the ear; the forehead also is less prominent and lower. Viewed in front, it is more or less pyramidal, being broad at the base and narrow at the top. Combativeness, Destructiveness, Acquisitiveness, Secretiveness, Cautiousness, and Constructiveness are generally full, as is also Imitation, while Causality, Ideality, and Mirthfulness are deficient. The face is broad and flat; the nose short and thick; the eyes black; the eyebrows very slight; the hair black and lank; the beard very slight, or entirely wanting; complexion tawny.

IV.—TEMPERAMENT IN THE MALAY RACE (Fig. 90).

It is not unlikely that the Malay is a cross, in which is mingled the blood of three distinct races—the Caucasian, the Mongolian, and the Ethiopian, and therefore not entitled to be considered as a distinct race. Be that as it may, he shows some of the characteristics of the Caucasian combined with traits which belong to the lower types mentioned. His skull is higher, and not so broad as that of the Mongolian, and he sometimes presents a facial angle not much inferior to that of the average Caucasian, but generally there is a projection of the jaws and a fullness of the lips which seem to ally him to the Negro. The features are prominent; the eyes and hair black; the complexion tawny, sometimes approaching the hue of mahogany. The Temperament is generally Bilious-Motive, the muscular development being more decided in the arms and chest than in the lower limbs, owing doubtless to the maritime habits of the race.

The Malay is active, enterprising, subtle, excitable, crafty, unprincipled, treacherous, sensual, and cruel. He is subject to fits of ungovernable passion, brought on by the use of alcoholic liquors, opium, and *bang* (smoking-hemp), in which he seems to thirst for blood and to be utterly insensible to either fear or bodily pain. This frenzy is known by the name of *Muck* or *Mook* in Sumatra, and *Wade* in India. To the same frenzy and nervous insensibility may be ascribed the ferocious, unyielding spirit manifested by the Malays in battle. "They fight to the last gasp; never ask and scarcely will accept quarter, or express thanks for mercy or the cure of wounds."

"The Malay," it has been aptly said, "is at once the tiger and the serpent of the East."

V.—TEMPERAMENT IN THE AMERICAN RACE
(Fig. 91).

In the American Indian we find the most perfect examples of the dark or bilious type of the Motive Temperament, or as we have more compactly expressed the constitutional condition referred to—the Bilious-Motive Temperament, shown in his tall, sinewy frame, muscular limbs, prominent features, harsh expression, black hair, black or brown eyes, and copper-colored complexion, as well as in his mental character, in which energy, persistence, firmness, dignity, bravery, cautiousness, cunning, and cruelty are marked traits. His cranium is heavy and coarse, and distinguished for its roundness, manifest in every aspect, for its great breadth immediately above the ears, and for a lofty coronal region. The forehead is broad, but retreating, showing the Perceptive faculties to predominate over the reasoning powers.

The Vital Temperament is sometimes, though rarely, found among the Indians, but the Mental is unknown among the uncivilized tribes.

VI.—TEMPERAMENT IN THE ETHIOPIAN RACE
(Fig. 92).

The tribes and nations of this race are widely dispersed, in Africa, Abyssinia, Australia, Borneo, and several other islands of the Indian Archipelago and in North and South America. The various tribes differ widely from each other, though all possessing certain general characteristics in common. We shall base our remarks under this head upon the Negro of our Southern States, as we find him to-day, after a

9*

few generations of slavery and a few years of freedom and franchise among civilized Caucasians. He has improved somewhat, even under the unfavorable conditions to which he has been subjected, but in the distinctive characteristics of his race, he is essentially the same as his brother in the interior of Africa.

The Temperament of the Negro is naturally Bilious-Motive, but examples of the Bilious-Vital are not uncommon, especially among the women; and the Sanguine element, though not often predominant, is by no means deficient, as the ample chest and active circulatory system attest. The influence of this last-named constitutional condition is seen in the lively, ardent, amiable, excitable, impulsive, and volatile disposition so often manifested under circumstances particularly calculated to draw them out; but the true basis of the Negro character, contrary to the generally received opinion, is laid more deeply in slow, steady energy and patient endurance. The American freedmen of to-day are oftener grave than gay, and are capable of undertaking the most serious enterprises and of carrying them out to the end—be that end success or failure—with a persistence for which they have not hitherto received credit. They are not good, however, in planning their undertakings, and their energy and pluck are generally thrown away. With all his amiability, sympathy, and real kindness of heart, the Negro can be guilty of the greatest cunning, ferocity, and cruelty.

The Mental Temperament is seldom found in the Negro, but will doubtless be hereafter developed by culture.

FIG. 91.—AMERICAN INDIAN.

FIG. 92.—THE NEGRO.

PLATE XLIV.

XV.

STUDIES IN TEMPERAMENT.

I.—THE GREAT TRAGEDIENNE (Fig. 93).

ANY careful reader of the foregoing chapters, having before him a head and face like the one here represented, will be able to determine at a glance the Temperament of the person to whom it belongs. The pyriform outline, the clearly-defined, sharply-cut features, the expression of lively intelligence, all indicate dominant mentality. On this simple fact he may base a tolerably correct general estimate of character, so far as character depends upon or is denoted by a constitutional condition. This is a marked case. There can be no question as to which system of organs is in the ascendant in the constitution. But even here, we must not be too hasty in summing up. The subordinate temperamental ele ments are to be taken into the account as well as the leading one. The practical difficulty lies in accurately measuring the relative proportion which each bears to the others, so as to assign to each its due influence on the character. Especially is it important to determine correctly which stands next to the leading one, in development and activity. In the case of Rachel, there was a solidity and firmness of texture

about her rather slight frame—a certain wiriness and
tension in her muscles—which hardly needed the testimony of her wondrous dark brown eyes and black
hair to prove the influential position of the Bilious-
Motive element in her constitution; and we know
that the effect must have been to strengthen and intensify all the natural manifestations of the Mental
Temperament. The refined tastes, the clear and correct artistic conceptions, the vivid and quick-coming
fancies, the ready discrimination, and the keen sensitiveness which characterize predominant brain-
power were here reinforced by the greater energy of
character, strength of will, firmness, and persistence
which belong to the system next in development and
activity. From the same source came the strong
passions, the overmastering ambition, and the impatience of wholesome restraint which sometimes
disturbed the current of a life immortalized by
genius. Without this potential tempering with the
bilious-muscular · element, however, Rachel could
never have become the Queen of Tragedy, though
she might have still had a brilliant career in some
other department of intellectual effort. It was this
which gave her the power to feel, appreciate, and
imbue herself with the passions she sought to portray
and to make them living realities on the stage.

II.—THE MORMON LEADER (Fig. 94).

A broad chest, a stout body, massive limbs, a full,
ruddy face indicate at once to the eye the predominance of the vital system, but a large, active brain
and a good development of the muscular or locomo-

FIG. 93.—RACHEL.

FIG. 94. BRIGHAM YOUNG.

PLATE XLV.

tive system (more evident in a photograph now before us than in th's engraving), temper this vigorous animality, with a high degree of intellectual power, energy of character, and executive ability. With a smaller brain, he might have been a mere vulgar sensualist; with less of the Motive element, he would have taken a subordinate place instead of becoming the chief ruler of his people. The basis of his character lay in his massive trunk, the never-failing source of that vital affluence which sustains, vivifies, warms, and quickens body and brain alike. The superstructure had the strength of sinew and the force of character imparted by the muscular constitution, and the intellectual ability and moral influence which come from a strongly-developed and well-balanced mental organization. The base of the brain was heavy and the neck short and thick, giving the Propensities great power and activity, but the high coronal region furnished the strong will and the high moral principles calculated to hold them measurably in check.

III.—The Daughter of a Queen (Fig. 95).

There is no lack of vital stamina in the Royal Family of England. The Queen, the Princes, and the Princesses all fitly represent the physical opulence the abounding vigor of the Anglo-Saxon race. The fullness of contour, the shapeliness of limb, the roundness of cheek, the freshness of complexion, which betoken good digestion, full respiration and rapid, equable circulation, are never lacking.

The Vital Temperament in the Princess Alice is sufficiently modified by a good mental development

to give considerable delicacy to the features, refinement to the manners, good taste and love of art and
literature, without detracting from the genial good-
nature, the lively animal spirits, the impulsiveness,
the ardor, and the amiable and affectionate disposition natural to it. The Motive element is but moderately developed, its principal indication, so far as
shown in our engraving, being the prominence of the
nose, which indicates some force of character and
steadiness of purpose.

IV.—A Savage Chieftain (Fig. 96).

Here is a type of the Red Man and of the dark or
Bilious-Motive Temperament. Large, dense bones;
heavy joints, like hinges of iron bound with bands
of steel; firm, wiry muscles; harsh, prominent features; high cheek-bones; retreating forehead; beetling
brows; deep-set, cruel, black eyes; coarse black hair;
and a hard, stern expression of countenance, are some
of the external indications of the great physical
strength, toughness, and endurance of this constitutional condition, as well as of its strong, rough, un-
compromising, energetic, steadfast, cool, calculating,
persistent mental character, softened by no human
tenderness, refined by no æsthetic tastes, and warmed
by no kindly impulses. Such a man is not likely to
show any amiable weaknesses, or to be turned aside
from any course he may have marked out for himself,
by sentimental considerations. He will shrink from
no danger which may lie in his path, and will endure
hardship and pain with indifference, if they come to
him in the pursuit of his ends. Sufferings inflicted

FIG. 95.—PRINCESS ALICE.

FIG. 96.—KANOSH, AN INDIAN CHIEF.

PLATE XLVI.

upon others will move him as little. Ambitious, fond of power, self-reliant, cool, cautious, secretive, brave, energetic, persevering, hard, stern, cruel, relentless—such is the Motive Temperament in the Savage, where the modifying influences of intellectual and moral culture are unfelt. There is here, keen observation, clear perceptions, shrewd common sense, immovable firmness, and considerable executive ability and talent for leading and controlling others, but little imagination, taste, or capacity for abstract reasoning.

V.—A SAVAGE WOMAN AND CHILD (Fig. 97).

This Polynesian woman presents a striking contrast to the Indian chief noted in the preceding section. Savages they both are, with dark skins and black eyes, but they are as unlike in Temperament as possible, and as unlike in character. Here we have the Vital constitution in its *melanic* form, or the Bilious-Vital Temperament, neither the Motive nor the Mental elements having an influential development. Light-hearted (as well as light-headed); luxuriating in all the mere animal enjoyments; good-natured, affectionate, impulsive, passionate, excitable, and volatile—such a being is constitutionally fitted to be the denizen of a lovely tropical island, resting in the bosom of peaceful seas, such as Pedro Fernandes de Quiros, the navigator who discovered Espiritu Santo in 1605, describes that delightful spot to be. He says:

"The rivers Jordan and Salvador give no small beauty to their shores, for they are full of odoriferous flowers and plants. Pleasant and agreeable groves

front the sea in every part ; we mounted to the tops
of mountains and perceived fertile valleys and rivers
winding among green meadows. The whole is a
country which, without doubt, has the advantage
over those of America, and the best of the European
will be well if it is equal. It is plenteous of various and delicious fruits, potatoes, yams, plantains,
oranges, limes, sweet basil, nutmegs, and ebony, all
of which, without the help of sickle, plow, or other
artifice, it yields in every season. There are also
cattle, birds of many kinds and of charming notes,
honey-bees, parrots, doves, and partridges. The
houses wherein the Indians live are thatched and
low, and they (the Indians, not the houses) are of a
black complexion."

Animals can not smile, nor have they, probably,
any sense of the ludicrous or the comic. Savages in
general have but a moderate or small development
of Mirthfulness, but our Polynesian woman has the
suggestion of a smile playing about her good-natured
mouth, and the baby would laugh if not too shy. It
is well-developed in some of the negroes of the Southern States.

Compare the Bilious-Vital Temperament in the
savage woman of Espiritu Santo with the light or
Sanguine type of the same constitution, as modified
by a large and active brain and the culture of a high
civilization, in the distinguished Irishwoman here
represented (Fig. 98). In the latter we recognize the
same full, rounded contours, general plumpness, and
breadth of development, as in the former, but the
impression of the whole organization is entirely dif-

FIG. 97.—NATIVES OF ESPIRITU SANTO.

FIG. 98.—LADY MORGAN.

PLATE XLVII.

ferent. The forehead has expanded, the eyes beam
with intelligence, the outlines of the features, though
softened and roundly curved, are clear and well-defined, and the expression is thoughtful and sympathetic. A different spirit looks out from behind the
mask of warm flesh and blood. Lady Morgan (Sid-
ney Owenson) once described herself as having "a
Temperament as cheery and genial as ever went to
that strange medley of pathos and humor—the Irish
character."

VI.—A WORKING BISHOP (Fig 99).

With the locomotive or osseous and muscular system well-developed, to give the heavy frame and
angular projections to the figure, and, at the same
time, an ample manifestation of the vital or nutritive
system, to fill out the skeleton with good solid flesh,
and to sustain the whole in vigorous action, we
observe a degree of squareness about the face, as
imperfectly shown in Fig. 99, in which, with a predominance of the Mental element, we have a strong
development of both the Motive and the Vital, forming a powerful organization for practical work, as
well as for observation, investigation, study, and
thought. Such a man is born to command and to
lead and control men, by the simple virtue of a calm,
cool, steady, energetic, self-reliant, determined character, backed up by a vigorous intellect, and a rich,
warm, and, at the same time, dense and tough
physical system. At the head of an army, or a
chairman of a church convention, he would show the

same self-control and the same mastery over those
around him.

Fig. 103 shows how a similar combination of temperamental elements is modified in expression by sex
and education.   Mrs. Clemmer, we are told, has dark
hair and blue eyes.   The former, with the strong,
prominent features and somewhat severe expression,
indicates the influence of the Motive constitution,
while the latter represents, in connection with a moderate fullness of cheeks and lips, the Sanguine or
Vital element, while there is sufficient expansion of
forehead, elevation of the coronal region, and clear-
cut sharpness in the features to show the dominance
of the brain-power.   She should be, as she is, a
ready, vigorous writer, as well as a keen, critical
observer.

VII.—A SOLID, STABLE CHARACTER (Fig. 100).

This portrait illustrates that class of cases referred
to in Chapter VII., in which age brings with it, in
the Vital and Mental-Vital Temperaments, a tendency to that constitutional condition described by
the pathologists as the Lymphatic Temperament.
Though to a certain extent an abnormal condition,
it is by no means inconsistent with endurance and
longevity—in fact, it may promote the latter by re-
tarding the too great activity of body and mind,
which so often hastens the wearing out of the physical system, and by promoting a calm, cool, dispas-
sionate state of mind, a love of ease, and a distaste
for the disturbing excitements of public life and the
cares and responsibilities of business.   In this case

FIG. 99.—BISHOP EASTBURN.

FIG. 100.—JOHN S. DARCY

PLATE XLVIII.

there is evidence of both vigor and toughness, great
tenacity of life, and a quiet, equable, well-regulated
disposition, eminently favorable to health and longevity. Dr. Franklin, and, to a lesser extent, General
Washington manifested the same lymphatic tendencies in old age.

Mr. Darcy's character, as delineated several years
ago in the *American Phrenological Journal,* is shown
to be a strong, practical, harmonious one, as the balance of temperamental conditions in his organization
would lead us to infer. "There is," the examiner
says, "decision, stability, and executiveness indicated, together with excellent planning talent; and
if he is not an inventor, he is capable of planning,
contriving, projecting, and devising ways and means
to accomplish difficult ends. He always makes his
brain save his hands. He is a man of comparatively
few words, but is full of thought and originality. He
is eminently kind, sympathetic, just, and devotional.
He is not brilliant, showy, imaginative, or poetical;
but kind, affectionate, watchful, and considerate.
Utility first, beauty and finish afterward, would be
his motto; though he would be tasteful, refined,
neat, and tidy, requiring and observing method and
order in all things. He has excellent judgment in
regard to the value of property, knowing exactly
what a dollar is worth, and what can be done with
it. He would make an excellent appraiser. He is
always manly and dignified without ostentation; has
a strong will without obstinacy; deep religious emotions without bigotry; is cautious without being timid,
and playful, mirthful, and joyous without hilarity."

VIII.—TEMPERAMENT "IN THE ROUGH" (Fig. 101).

Here the Vital Temperament (in the daughter) and the Vital-Motive (in the mother) are represented in the rough aspect in which they manifest themselves among the rude, uncultivated lower class of a European sea-port—not lower in vitality and strength of constitution, but in intellectual development and cultivation. Observe what large, muscular bodies, large necks, and moderate-sized brains. The business of this class is to live and enjoy life in the affections and senses rather than in the intellect or sentiments. All the bodily functions are healthy and vigorous— digestion, breathing, and circulation. Without the luxuries of the higher circles of life, they subsist upon the simplest food, live much in the open air, and enjoy life into extreme old age. These are simple-minded, temperate, and virtuous people, whose wants are few, and who live nearer to nature than many in more fashionable circles. They are profoundly religious, full of faith, hope, and trust, with limited education, see a Providence even in calamities, and accept reverses and disappointments without a murmur. They are full of life, and happy in their condition. The mother has a resolute, determined expression, is very self-reliant and energetic, and will, we may be sure, turn aside from her course for no one. Strong-willed, severe (when severity may be required) and perhaps domineering, she is still, by virtue of the influential activity of the strong vital element in her constitution, kind, benevolent, and sympathetic.

FIG. 101.—FISHERWOMEN OF BOULOGNE.

FIG. 102.—MRS. LOUISA CHANDLER MOULTON.

FIG. 103.—MARY CLEMMER.

PLATE XLIX

The daughter is of a softer and more pliable organization, and will yield to the pressure of circumstances, where resistance might involve pain, hardship, or self-sacrifice. In her disposition she is more pleasing and amiable.

Though these simple fisherwomen have little more intellectual development or training than savages, they are far above them in the scale of being, through the reflected light of the civilization which shines around them, and the purer religion which has elevated their moral sentiments and refined their affections.

IX.—A LITERARY LADY (Fig. 102).

From a fisherwoman of Boulogne to a cultivated and refined American lady is a long step, and great is the difference between the organic quality of the two, though both have the same general configuration and are made up of similar materials—bones, muscles, tissues, and fluids. The one is coarse, the other fine. Here we have delicacy, grace, and beauty; there rough outlines, awkward movements, and homely features. In the lady, the chiseling is clear and sharp; in the fish-wife, blurred and broken. In the latter, the animal nature predominates; in the former the mental.

Mrs. Moulton has the Mental Temperament, with sufficient of the vital element to impart a good degree of warmth, amiability, impulsiveness, and buoyancy to her disposition and give liveliness, brilliancy, and versatility to her intellectual efforts; and enough of the Motive to endow her with the necessary toughness of physical fiber and stability of moral character.   Her eyes are probably gray or hazel, her hair dark brown, and her complexion between fair and dark.   "She is a pleasing and entertaining writer, and is always affable, gracious, and overflowing with courtesy; has a quick and appreciative eye for whatever is beautiful in poetry or prose, in art or in nature, and delights far more in pointing out the merits of an author than in holding him up to even deserved censure."   So an admirer says of her, and her organization does not falsify the estimate of the friendly pen.

X.—An Ardent, Emotional Character (Fig. 104).

No one will need to be told that we have here a representation of the Vital Temperament.   The nutritive functions are in fact rather excessive in their action, giving a superabundance of all the life-sustaining elements and an undesirable fullness to the figure—a plumpness bordering on corpulence.   A good intellectual endowment, however, redeems the lady's organization from any suspicion of mere animal grossness.   Another feature of her constitution, not so obvious, perhaps, to the casual observer, in an uncolored picture, imparts an air of solidity and strength to her person and of force and dignity to her character.   This is the *melanic* or bilious element indicated by dark eyes, black hair, and a peachy bloom on the cheek.   She should be a good observer and by no means deficient as a thinker; should converse fluently and well, and be full of emotion and passion.

FIG. 104.—MARTHA HAINES BUTTS BENNETT.

FIG. 105.—A NEGRO.

PLATE L.

She is warm, ardent, voluptuous, sympathetic, and enthusiastic, but at the same time earnest, self-poised, and firm. "When such a nature takes the offensive, there is no half-way work. She is resolute as well as tender; executive, but not cruel or vindictive; cautious, but not timid or irresolute; self-relying, but not haughty. She loves her liberty, and will not submit to restraint, but can conform and adapt herself to circumstances. She may be led or persuaded, but can not be driven." She probably owes the *melanic* element in her constitution to a strain of Celtic blood, being of French descent on the mother's side.

The influence of the dark or bilious element when associated with the Vital Temperament, forming what we have called the Bilious-Vital Temperament, has received too little attention and should be carefully studied by the physiologist as well as by the reader of character.

XI.—THE MELANIC OR DARK ELEMENT (Fig. 105).

Like the great majority of his race, this Negro has the Motive Temperament, shown by the projecting cheek bones and jaws, and (inferentially) the length and size of the bones generally, as well as by the length of the cranium, which would be found also thick and dense. The osseous and muscular systems are decidedly predominant, but there is no marked deficiency in the nutritive system, the breathing power and circulation being good, and the digestion admirable.

The Mental Temperament is almost unknown

among the Negroes of the Southern States of the
Union, but will, no doubt, be developed as one of
the results of freedom, franchise, and free schools.
The Vital Temperament is common enough among
the women employed as house servants, nurses, etc.,
but " field hands " of both sexes—generally the descendants of generations of " field hands "—inherit
the muscular development which is the basis of the
Motive Temperament.

The supposed light-hearted, buoyant, jovial, careless, and improvident character of the Negro has
seemed to indicate a sanguine constitution or Vital
Temperament. All Southern races are improvident
and lacking in forethought in matters pertaining to
the shelter and sustenance of the body; not from the
effects of a volatile Temperament, but because nature
and climate are too opulent and deal too generously
with them to render industrious, careful, and saving
habits necessary. As to any peculiar gay, rollicking,
light-heartedness, and love of pleasure in the Negro
character it is a mere fiction of the casual observer,
probably growing out of the fact that in the time of
slavery, dancing, music, singing, and wild revelry
marked festive occasions among them. These were
reactions against the monotonous labors and close
restraints of their condition, and no indications of the
general tone of feeling among them. These scenes
have almost entirely disappeared, since "freedom
came," giving place to political and religious meet-
ings, processions, and other more serious relaxations.
In fact, the prevailing tone is a grave one, evincing
far more pathos than hilarity. All genuine Negro

music is in the minor key, and neither slavery nor freedom have thus attuned their voices. There is in them a toughness, a power of sustained action, and a persistence of purpose, as well as a slow movement and a cool, calculating policy which belong to the Melano-Motive Temperament alone.

XII.—An American Soldier (Fig. 106).

This portrait represents a fine example of the Motive-Mental Temperament, the prominences and angularities of the strong osseous system being somewhat smoothed down, sharpened, and refined by the full development and great activity of the brain and nervous system.

General Logan is described as being "tall and tough, with a most flexible physiology; his hair is black and wiry; his skin a reddish-white or a livid brown; eyes full, black, and piercing; nose prominent; nostrils large; chin long and projecting; jaws strong and well set on; mouth large, but well cut; lips full and firm; ears above the average, and the neck is large and sinewy. His breathing, circulation, and digestion are excellent."

In character, he is cool, brave, self-reliant, unaffected, firm, self-possessed, independent, proud, strong-willed, energetic, clear-headed, persevering, somewhat severe, if not stern, but at the same time warm-hearted and sympathetic. As a friend, he may be counted on under all circumstances, for he is eminently steadfast and constant; as an enemy he would be bitter and perhaps cruel and unrelenting. His intellectual abilities are above the average, but his

10

efficiency is largely due to his energetic Temperament. " He would have made a capital engineer, explorer, navigator, or a pioneer. He is careless of mere ornament, but values the substantials. His Ideality is not large, and love of the beautiful is subordinate to his sense of the useful."

XIII.—CHIEF OF THE HORSEMEN (Fig. 107).

Here we have the Mental-Motive Temperament, the Motive element being of the strong dark type, indicated by the brown or black eyes, black hair, nut-brown complexion, and prominent and somewhat harsh features, softened in expression by the mental influences so active in the organization.

General Sheridan is energetic, tenacious of purpose, self-reliant, ambitious, prompt in action, cool, brave, trustworthy, clear-headed, quick to comprehend the situation and impetuous in execution. His intellect is of the practical kind, and manifests itself most efficiently in emergencies, when less cool and self-poised minds are thrown off their balance and are powerless to meet the demands of the hour.

A newspaper correspondent describes Gen. Sheridan as follows:

"There is no waste timber about Sheridan; not much of him physically, but snugly put together. A square face, a warm, black eye, a pleasant smile, a reach of under jaw, showing that 'when he will, he will, you may depend on't;' black hair, trimmed round like a garden-border; no Hyperion curl about him any more than there was about Cromwell's troopers· and altogether impressing you with the

FIG. 106.—JOHN A. LOGAN.

FIG. 107.—GEN. PHILIP SHERIDAN.

PLATE LI.

truth that there is about as much energy packed away in about the smallest space that you ever saw in your life. Men ranging down from medium size to little, with exceptions enough to prove the rule, seem to carry the day among the heroes. Moses was something of a General, but no Falstaff; Alexander the Great and Peter the Great were little; Cromwell was no giant, and as for Napoleon—why, what was he but 'the little Corporal?' Sheridan is a capital executive officer; perhaps he would be hardly equal to planning a great campaign; but, Jehu! wouldn't he *drive* it! With a good piece of his head behind his ears, and hardly reverence enough for a mandarin, he is not afraid of the face of clay. As chief of cavalry, he is indeed chief among ten thousand."

XVI.

TEMPERAMENT IN THE LOWER ANIMALS.

WE find, in the lower animals—at least in such of them as we purpose to include in this sketch—the same grand systems of organs as in man—the locomotive or mechanical system; the Vital or nutritive system; and the Mental or nervous system. These are combined in different proportions, in the different species of animals, and to a limited extent in different individuals of the same species. The lower animals may, therefore, be said to have the same Temperaments as are found in the human family, or, at least, to have the capacity for the same mixing or tempering of the constitution with the three primitive elements—Motive, Vital, and Mental.

I.—TEMPERAMENT IN WILD ANIMALS (Figs. 108 to 115).

In speaking of the savage races we have had occasion to remark that there is a degree of uniformity in Temperament not found among civilized peoples, nearly all the individuals of the same race having a similar constitution. Among wild animals this uniformity is almost perfect. Every tiger (Fig. 112) has the Bilious-Motive Temperament, though there may be individual differences in the strength of its devel-

FIG. 108.—LION

FIG. 109.—BEAR.

FIG. 110.—WOLF

FIG. 111.—FOX.

FIG. 114.—EAGLE.

FIG. 113.—DEER.

FIG. 112.—TIGER.

FIG. 115.—ANTELOPE

TEMPERAMENT IN WILD ANIMALS.

PLATE LII.

opment; every opossum has the Vital Temperament, and every deer (Fig. 113) the Mental or Nervous Temperament. When we come to speak of the common domestic animals, we shall see that the case is quite different. Man has here interfered with the regular working of natural laws, causing many modifications of the most singular and interesting character in the original Temperament and configuration of the horse, the ox, the sheep, etc. The law in such cases seems to be that the higher the organization and the greater the culture, the more numerous and wider the individual differences.

The lion (Fig. 108), the wolf (Fig. 110), and the carnivorous animals generally, have, like the tiger, the Motive or Bilious, or, in our nomenclature, the Bilious-Motive Temperament, and are blood-thirsty, cunning, treacherous, and cruel. The bear (Fig. 109) has a larger development of the nutritive system than the tiger, the wolf, etc., and may be described as having the Motive-Vital Temperament. He is by no means exclusively a flesh-eater, but is very fond of fruits and of honey, and takes on fat readily. The intelligence of the lion and of the fox may perhaps entitle them to the distinction of having ascribed to them the Motive-Mental Temperament. In the latter (Fig. 111) the shapely face and sharp, clear-cut features seem to indicate such a combination of the temperamental elements. Cautiousness and Secretiveness, and especially the latter, are remarkably developed in the fox.

In the grass-eating or herbivorous tribes, we find the muscular or locomotive system generally less

powerfully developed, either the vital or the nervous
assuming the ascendency. Thus the deer and the
antelope (Figs. 113 and 115) have the Mental or
Nervous Temperament, and the woodchuck and the
beaver have the Vital, though in the latter the muscular system is still very powerful.

Among the feathered tribes the same general law
holds good. Birds of prey, like the eagle, the hawk,
and the owl, are powerfully developed in bone and
muscle, but thin of flesh, and never fat, while the
seed-eaters, like the grouse, the quail, and the wild
pigeon, are inclined to plumpness and quickly become fat, where food suited to their wants is abundant. The latter have the Vital Temperament; the
former, with the swallows, night-hawks, and other
swift-flying, insect-eating birds, have the Motive.

II.—TEMPERAMENT IN DOMESTIC ANIMALS.

We now come in contact with various artificial
conditions, such as diet, breeding, and training,
through which almost numberless modifications of
the original types have been produced in the species
of animals which have long been subjected to man.
We no longer find that uniformity which, in the wild
animals, enables us, in discussing Temperament, to
ignore the individual and speak only of species. In
horses, cattle, sheep, swine, etc., we must discriminate
between the different races, breeds, and varieties, and
even note individual differences, as indications of
mental and temperamental peculiarities.

1. *The Horse* (Figs. 116 to 121).—The original
Temperament of the horse, unlike that of the grass-

eaters generally, was probably the Motive, or possibly Motive-Vital. The wild horses still to be found on the Asiatic side of the Volga, and stretching thence over the boundless wilds of the interior, are thus described:

"Their heads are large, thick, and very convex above the eyes; their ears are long, habitually carried low, and hanging backward; their limbs are long, but stout; the muzzle thick and garnished with bristles, and long hairs grow beneath the jaws and under part of the neck. The hair of the body is long and shaggy, sometimes frizzled. The color is usually brownish-dun, approaching to a muddy cream-color. These horses are gregarious, and are often seen in numbers of several hundred together."

Catching and subduing the original wild horse, or horses (for it is not known whether all our races and breeds of this animal are descended from one original stock or from several), man has, by selection and systematic breeding, produced a great variety in constitution and configuration. Here, giving length and slenderness of limb for speed and ease of action, as in the race-horse; there, developing bone and muscle, as in the Clydesdale (Fig 116).

In the horse, whether bred for the saddle, the carriage, or for heavy draught — whether we desire slenderness or grace, or stoutness and strength, it is dense, wiry muscle that we aim at, and not cellular tissue and fat; so the vital system has been diminished so far as health and the necessary capacity for nutrition will permit. Our training also has had its influence, developing the brain, increasing the intelli-

gence, and encouraging the nervous or mental system.
The result is a great variety of constitutional conditions, but none of them tending to a complete preponderance of the nutritive or vital system. The
Temperaments in the domestic horse vary from the
typical Motive or Motive-Vital of the wild animal to
the Nervous or Mental in the Arabian and some of
his grades.

The characteristics of the different Temperaments
in animals are similar to those observed in man, so
far as the difference between us and the lower animals
permits comparison. In the Motive Temperament
there are always large bones, strong, dense, wiry muscles, and a configuration strongly marked and inclined
to angularity; in the Vital, relatively smaller bones,
more plumpness and more gracefully rounded forms;
in the Mental, slenderness, sharpness of outline, and
delicacy and fineness of texture.

In Fig. 118 we have the Motive Temperament and
a headstrong, combative, obstinate, and unyielding
disposition. A stronger development of the vital and
mental systems would have greatly improved his
temper and capacity. Fig. 120 represents such a
modification and a high degree of intelligence, docility, and gentleness, indicated by width between the
eyes, prominence of those organs, and roundness and
elevation between and above them. Figs. 117 and
119 represent the Nervous or Mental Temperament
and great activity and intelligence; but Fig. 117 is
timid, restive, and excitable, and needs coolness, calmness, and patience in his management. Fig. 119 is
rather sly, cunning, mischievous, and untrustworthy.

FIG. 116.—THE CLYDESALE HORSE.

FIG. 117.

FIG. 118.

FIG. 1 9.

FIG. 120.

FIG. 121.

TEMPERAMENT IN HORSES,

PLATE LIII.

For the cart or dray, and for cavalry service, the hard, tough muscles and powerful organization of the Motive Temperament are desirable, but there should be a sufficient development of the Mental system to give a fair degree of intelligence and enough of the Vital to insure a good digestion and a facility to keep in good flesh. For the saddle and light draught on the road, we want more of the mental element to give slenderness, grace, and ease of action. A good serviceable family horse, for all kinds of work and for the use of boys and women, should have a good balance of temperamental conditions and a head like Fig. 120.

The abnormal condition described as the Lymphatic Temperament is not unknown among horses and is characterized by a lazy, sluggish disposition and an entire absence of the pride, spirit, and ambition which are natural to the well-constituted and healthy animal.

A certain degree of development of the vital system, and especially of the sanguine element, represented by the depth and breadth of the chest, are essential in every horse to which we look for continued labor, whether under the saddle, in the light wagon, buggy, or phaeton, in the carriage, or for heavy draught. In the race-horse alone, there may be a disproportionate slenderness of body and length of limb, inconsistent with long-continued effort or steady labor.

Horses with well-balanced Temperaments are the most healthy and long-lived, and will do the greatest amount of work with the least outlay of strength, as

10*

their bodies, limbs, and brains are in harmony with
each other, and perfect symmetry exists throughout,
conducive of ease of action, as well as evenness of
temper and a gentle, quiet disposition.

Some of the points of a horse, as they are more
or less matters of Temperament, will not be out of
place here :

(1). The head should be symmetrical and not too
large, as a very large head in a horse generally indicates thick, heavy bones and a dull, sluggish constitution.   There should be a good forehead, however,
the points of which have already been stated.

(2). The ears should be fine, pointed, and erect.
Horses with lopping ears are not necessarily bad, but
they are apt to be slow and dull.

(3). The eyes should be large and prominent and
the eyelids thin.

(4). The nostrils should be expansive. They are indicative of the sanguine element of the constitution,
of breathing power, and consequently of speed. Narrow nostrils are entirely inconsistent with rapid
movement.

(5). The neck should be of medium length and
somewhat arched or convex.

(6). There must be a roomy chest, for well-developed
lungs and full breathing power; but where speed is
required, this room should be obtained by extension
in depth rather than in breadth, as a broad chest sets
the fore legs too far apart for ease of action. For
heavy draught, the chest should be broad.

(7). The back should be elevated at the withers, as
indicating ease of action in the fore legs. A straight

back indicates strength; a long back is a sign of speed, and a short one of strength and endurance. The latter is usually associated with short legs, a round, plump body, and a marked combination of the Vital and Motive Temperaments.

(8). The ribs should be well curved, so that the sides shall not be flat and the body narrow, as this conformation indicates deficient vital stamina and endurance.

(9). The haunches or quarters should be well expanded in every direction, as they indicate the power of progression. In all animals, the power of rapid motion is in direct relation with the development of the posterior extremities, as in the greyhound, the deer, and the antelope.

(10). All the limbs should be symmetrical and in harmony with the form of the body and the Temperament and uses of the animal.

Always examine the heads, faces, and expressions of animals before buying. The temperamental and physiognomical signs are as applicable to them as to men.

2. *Cattle* (Fig. 122).—In cattle and other animals domesticated and bred mainly for the production of human food, the effort has naturally been to produce an adaptation to the rapid production of flesh, together with the fatty secretions desired as articles of diet; and as the capacity to readily assimilate nourishment depends upon the development and activity of the digestive, respiratory, and circulatory organs, whose seat is in the great cavities of the trunk, and which constitute the Vital system, the result has been to make the

Vital Temperament almost universal among animals of this class. The production of milk in the cow and of wool on the sheep has, however, led to some modifications of this tendency.

The original wild stock from which our domestic cattle are derived, is still to be found pure and in the natural untamed state in some European parks, and descriptions of the animal show that there is a much more powerful development of the osseous and muscular systems than in our improved domestic breeds, though in other respects the difference is not very marked.

We may, then, set down the Temperament of our domestic cattle as generally strongly Vital, modified in some breeds, and notably in the Jersey, by a large infusion of the Mental or Nervous element, constituting the Vital-Mental, and in the half-wild cattle of the Southwest and of Florida by a partial return to the Vital-Motive constitution of the original stock.

In the case of the Jersey breed, several causes have led to their more delicate and deer-like nervous constitution. In the first place, they have been bred for many generations exclusively for dairy purposes, the idea of beef being ignored, or at least made entirely subservient to the production of milk and butter. This has naturally induced breeders to disregard the indications of the flesh-forming and fat-producing qualities in favor of those relating to milk secretion; secondly, the custom of soiling, or feeding in stables or small yards, generally followed in the Channel Islands, allowing the animals little exercise, has further diminished both the vital and the locomotive systems, while

FIG. 122.—A SHORT HORN BULL.

FIG. 123.—SHEEP.

FIG. 124.—HOG.

TEMPERAMENT IN DOMESTIC ANIMALS.

PLATE LIV.

it has increased the nervous; and, finally, the more perfectly domesticated condition in which these cattle are kept, the closer intimacy between them and their owners, and the petting to which they are subject, while diminishing their vital stamina, have increased their nervous tendencies and their intelligence.

The indications of the nervous constitution or Mental Temperament in cattle are similar to those of that condition in the horse—a comparative slimness of horns, neck, and tail; a clean, well-cut muzzle; finely modeled limbs, and an expression of vivacity and intelligence.

In cattle raised principally with a view to the production of flesh and fatty tissue, the chest should be both wide and deep, the trunk capacious, the bones relatively small, and the limbs tapering—in other words, the Temperament should be Vital.

The head should be rather small, but with considerable frontal development and breadth between the eyes, these being indications of intelligence, amiability, and docility. Great breadth of head is unfavorable, as a sign of an unruly and quarrelsome disposition; but the head of the bull is naturally broader than that of the cow, and any approach in the latter to the masculine configuration indicates a deficient capacity for producing milk.

The horns should be delicate and sharp rather than coarse and thick, but difference of breed must be taken into account in judging of their characteristics.

A short neck, another characteristic of the Vital Temperament, is a good point, but there is some-

times an undue shortness, detracting from symmetry
and rendering it difficult for the animal to feed from
the ground.

A capacious trunk being connected with a strong
vital system and a capacity for fattening, the ribs
should be widely arched, rising almost horizontally
from the spine, and then bending downward with a
sweep, producing a broad back, which should also be
nearly straight.   Although a short, compact body indicates robustness and capacity to fatten, a moderate
length is desirable, as adding to the weight and value
of the animal.

The haunches should be long and well expanded
in every direction, as they add largely to the weight of
the animal ; and, corresponding with the width of the
trunk, both the fore and hinder limbs will be far apart.

Whether in the side view, or seen from behind, the
ox or the cow, and still more the bull, should present
a square and massive aspect.

The skin should be soft to the touch, have an
unctuous feel, and be well covered with soft hair.

The points essential to the milk-producing capacity are connected mainly with the hinder parts.
The loins should be wide, and the trunk deep from
the loins to the mammæ.   This form existing, the
more a cow possesses of the other characteristics
enumerated, the better will she combine milking with
fattening qualities.   A purely dairy cow should have
a soft skin, clear eyes, a narrow, elongated head, a
good-sized udder, the superficial veins near which
should be well marked, and especially what is called
the " milk-vein."

We copy from a work on domestic animals the following complete list of points, from which it will be seen that the results of observation and experience accord with those we have deduced from physiological principles:

(1). The nose or muzzle in the Durhams or Short Horns should be of a rich cream-color. In the Devon, Hereford, and Sussex it is preferred when a clear golden color. A brown or dark color indicates a cross.

(2). The forehead should be neither narrow nor very broad. The eye should be prominent, and the nostril between the eye and the muzzle thin, particularly in the Devons.

(3). The horns should be small, smooth, tapering, and sharp-pointed, long or short, according to the breed, and of a white color throughout in some breeds, and tipped with black in others. The shape is less essential than the color.

(4). The neck should be of medium length, full at the sides, not too deep in the throat, and should come out from the shoulders nearly on a level with the chine.

(5). The top of the plate bones should not be too wide, but, rising on a level with the chine, should be well thrown back, so that there may be no hollowness behind.

(6). The shoulder-joint should lay flat with the ribs, without any projection.

(7). The breast should be wide and open, projecting forward.

(8). The chine should lay straight, and be well covered with flesh.

(9). The loin should be flat and wide; almost as wide at the fore as the hinder part.

(10). The hip-bones should be wide apart, coming upon a level with the chine to the setting of the tail.

(11). The tip of the rump should be tolerably wide, so that the tail may drop to a level between the two points; and the tail should come out broad.

(12). The thigh should not be too full outside nor behind; but the inside or twist should be full.

(13). The back should be flat and rather thin. ·

(14). The hind leg should be flat and thin; the legs of medium length, and the hock rather turning out.

(15). The feet should not be too broad.

(16). The flank should be full and heavy when the animal is fat.

(17). The belly should not drop below the breast, but on a line with it.

(18). The shoulder should be rather flat, not projecting.

(19). The fore-leg should also be flat and upright, but not fleshy.

(20). The round should not project, but be flat with the outside of the thigh.

(21). The jaws should be rather wide.

(22). The ribs should spring nearly horizontally from the chine and form a circle.

(23). The skin should be loose, floating, as it were, on a layer of soft fat, and covered with thick, glossy, soft hair.

(24). The expression of the eye and face should be calm and complacent.

A writer in the *Farmer's Magazine*, a number of years ago, described what are properly considered the good points of a cow, as exhibited in the Short Horn breed, in the following doggerel lines:

> She's long in her face, she's fine in her horn ;
> She'll quickly get fat without cake or corn ;
> She's clean in her jaws, and full in her chine ;
> She's heavy in flank, and wide in her loin ;
> She's broad in her ribs, and long in her rump ;
> She's straight in her back, with never a hump ;
> She's wide in her hip, and calm in her eyes ;
> She's fine in her shoulders, and thin in her thighs ;
> She's light in her neck, and small in her tail ;
> She's wide in her breast, and good at the pail ;
> She's fine in her bone, and silky of skin ;
> She's a grazier's without, and a butcher's within.

3. *The Sheep* (Fig. 123).—Little need be said of the temperamental characteristics of the sheep, except that the same general rules apply to all the different breeds as those we have given for cattle. It is the Vital Temperament that has been exclusively cultivated, and the configuration characteristic of that Temperament is what we look for in a good mutton sheep. All the improved breeds possess this, though some in a higher degree than others. The South-Down is perhaps the best mutton sheep in the world, so far at least as the quality of its flesh is concerned.

When sheep deteriorate, as they are sure to do under neglect, and as they have done in this country and elsewhere, it is always in the direction of the Motive Temperament, the bones becoming larger, the muscles denser, the limbs longer, and the general configuration more angular and homely; and this is doubtless an imperfect return toward the original physical character of the species.

4. *The Hog* (Fig. 124).—Doubtless the natural Temperament of the hog, as it exists in a wild state, is strongly Vital, though the muscular and osseous systems are also well developed and the character of the animal energetic, courageous, and fierce. The results of breeding in domestication, with special reference to the production of flesh, and especially of fatty tissue, have been to increase the natural vital tendency to an excess known in no other domestic animal, and to produce what we must consider an abnormal lymphatic condition inconsistent with health.

In hogs running in the woods and making their own living on the "root hog or die" principle, as at the South, there is, as in the case of the sheep, a partial return to the native wild constitution, in which the locomotive system gains development at the expense of the fat-forming capacity. The flesh of such hogs is less unwholesome than that of our improved and highly fattened animals; but of course there are big streaks of "lean" and heavy bones.

"There is evidently," the *Farmers' Cyclopedia* says, "much diversity in swine in different circumstances and situations. Like other descriptions of stock, they should be selected with especial reference to the nature of the climate, the keep, and the circumstances of the management under which the farm is conducted. The chief points to be consulted in judging of the breeds of this animal are the form or shape of the ear, and the quality of the hair. The pendulous or lop ear, and coarse, harsh hair, are commonly asserted to indicate largeness of size and thickness of skin; while erect or prick ears show the size to be smaller, but the animals to be more quick in feeding.

"In the selection of swine, the bes: formed are considered to be those which are not too long, but full in the head and cheek; thick and rather short in the neck; fine in the bone; thick, plump, and compact in the carcass; full in the quarters, fine and thin in the hide; and of a good size according to the breed, with, above all, a kindly disposition to fatten well and expeditiously at an early age. Depth of carcass, lateral extension, breadth of the loin and breast, proportionate length, moderate shortness of the legs, and substance of the gammons and forearms, are therefore absolute essentials. These are qualities to produce a favorable balance in the account of keep, and a mass of weight which will pull the scale down. In proportion, too, as the animal is capacious in the loin and breast, will be generally the vigor of his constitution; his legs will be thence properly distended, and he will have a bold and firm footing on the ground."

5. *The Dog* (Figs. 125–134).—The dog presents a greater variety in Temperament, configuration, and character than any other domestic animal. The Mastiff, powerful in muscle, tough, hardy, tenacious, watchful, and courageous, illustrates the Motive Temperament. The Bull-dog has also a very powerful locomotive system, but it is modified in him by a greater development of the vital system, giving the Motive-Vital Temperament and a fierce, indomitable, and

implacable disposition. In the Shepherd's dog we have a fine example of the Mental or Nervous Temperament. A strictly Vital Temperament is not, we believe, a natural condition in the dog, or in any other purely carnivorous animal, but is often superinduced in domestication, in any breed of a conformation favorable to the production of flesh and fatty tissue.

The races of domestic dogs have been arranged in three groups, as follows:

(1). The Lyciscan, or wolf-like Group;

(2). The Vertragral, or swift-footed Group;

(3). The Molossian, or Mastiff Group; and

(4). The Indigator, or scent-following Group.

(1). The Lyciscan Group of dogs comprises those races which inhabit the northern glacial regions and bear a general resemblance to the wolf. They are, as a group, considered the least removed from the natural state and have a strong preponderance of the osseous and muscular systems, or, in other words, the Motive Temperament. They are, in many cases, used as draught animals and drag heavy sledges over the snow and ice of the frozen regions they inhabit. They are generally fierce, treacherous, and vindictive, and their power of endurance is wonderful.

Savage and intractable as are the wolf-like dogs of the Esquimaux and the Laplanders (Fig. 131), we have before us positive proof that these animals are susceptible of high culture and the development of some of the noblest qualities of the canine genus. The Shepherd's dog (Figs. 126 and 129) clearly referable to this class, is now a gentle, docile, faithful, and (in the discharge of his peculiar functions) won-

FIG. 125.—MOTIVE.

FIG. 126.—MENTAL.

FIG. 127.—VITAL.

FIG. 128.—BULL-DOG.

FIG. 129.—SHEPARD.

FIG. 130.—POINTER.

FIG. 131.—ESQUIMAUX.

FIG. 132.—ST. BERNARD.

FIG. 133.—SPANIEL.

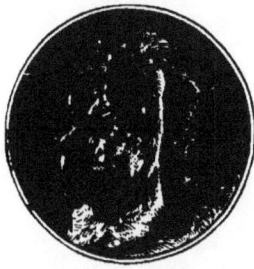

FIG. 134.—HOUND.

FIG. 135.—CAT.

TEMPERAMENT IN DOGS.

PLATE LV.

derfully sagacious animal. The wolf-like head, in its
general outlines, is still observable, but so softened,
refined, and elevated as to give it an entirely different expression and signification. The Temperament
is no longer Bilious-Motive, but Mental; and the
ferocity of the savage has given place to the patient
devotion of the servant and friend of man. Wonderful instances of their faithfulness and intelligence are
on record.

The noble and sagacious Newfoundland dog is believed to be a cross between an Esquimaux Lyciscan
dog and some large English breed, probably the
Mastiff.

(2). Of the Vertragral Group the lithe and graceful
Greyhound is the type. This dog varies much in
external characteristics, depending upon the circumstances under which he is reared and the manner
in which he is employed. Formerly, having been
habituated for generations to hunt the stag and
other large animals, he was larger in stature and far
more muscular than he is now generally seen, especially when reared in dwellings, as a pet. His
natural characteristics fitted him to follow his prey
by sight rather than scent and overtake it by his
great speed of foot. His Temperament, under normal conditions, is the Motive.

(3). The Molossian Group comprises the larger and
fiercer kinds of dogs, of which the Mastiff is the type.
This animal is extremely powerful and very fierce,
but docile and sagacious in the highest degree. He
is by hereditary endowment a watch-dog and most
vigilantly and faithfully does he perform his duty

He is not blood-thirsty, and, unless trained to mur-
der, is as forbearing as his duty to his master will
permit. For the thief or unlawful intruder there is
no escape, but if he make no resistance, the dog will
not harm him. He is slow to anger and submits
patiently to the teasing of children or of other and
smaller dogs.

The great St. Bernard dog (Fig. 132) belongs to
this group and is one of the noblest and most intelligent of all dogs. His head is finely developed and
his expression full of benignity. The Temperament
may be called Motive-Mental.

(4). The Indigator Group embraces the true hounds
(Fig. 134), and other scent-following hunting dogs, including the Pointer (Fig. 130), Setter, Spaniel (Fig.
133), and Terrier. These races, though classed together
on account of that quality of keen scent which makes
them so valuable as hunting dogs, are widely different from each other in configuration and Temperament, and consequently in disposition and intelligence. The Spaniel is the most intelligent of them
all, and the most docile and affectionate. "It will
never turn against its master, but lick the hand that
chastises it. Even the Arabs find an excuse for fond-
ling the Spaniel, asserting that it is not a dog." The
Spaniel has been largely mixed in blood with other
races, and many dogs bear the name which have little if any of the Spaniel blood.

6. *The Cat* (Fig. 135).—Like the tiger, the leopard,
and other members of the genus *Felis*, the cat has
naturally the Bilious-Motive Temperament, and the
hard, cruel, treacherous character associated with this

constitution in animals; but domestication and close intimacy, for centuries, with the human race, together with a partial change of diet, have modified to a limited extent its constitution, disposition, and habits, giving it often a Vital predominance and an amiable and ordinarily gentle disposition, accompanied with considerable intelligence and docility. It returns with great facility, however, to its wild habits, and its cautious, secretive, and destructive instincts are readily awakened.

A GREAT BOOK FOR YOUNG PEOPLE.

"CHOICE OF PURSUITS; or, What to Do and Why,"

Describing Seventy-five Trades and Professions, and the Temperaments and Talents required for each; With Portraits and Biographies of many successful Thinkers and Workers. By Nelson Sizer, President of the American Institute of Phrenology; author of "Forty Years in Phrenology;" "How To Teach According to Temperament and Mental Development," etc. Price, $1.50.

This work, "Choice of Pursuits," fills a place attempted by no other. Whoever has to earn a living by labor of head or of hand can not afford to do without it.

NOTICES OF THE PRESS.

"'CHOICE OF PURSUITS; or, What to Do and Why," is the title of a remarkable book. The author has attained a deserved eminence as a phrenological delineator of character. We have given it a careful reading and feel warranted in saying that it is a book calculated to do a vast deal of good."—*Boston Commonwealth.*

"It presents many judicious counsels for the conduct of life. The main purpose of the writer is to prevent mistakes in the choice of a profession. His remarks on the different trades are often highly original. The tendency of this volume is to increase the reader's respect for human nature."--*New York Tribune.*

"The design of this book is to indicate to every man his own proper work, and to educate him for it. The author's observations are sound."—*Albany Evening Journal.*

"We like this book; we wish people would read it; we wish editors and preachers would read it. One very great evil which this book is well calculated to mitigate is the tumbling of people into pursuits for which they have no gifts. The hints are many and really valuable."—*Newark Daily Journal.*

The most important step in life is the selecting of the pursuit for which one's faculties, temperaments, and education best adapt him. The young man or woman who makes the right selection is guaranteed thereby a happy and successful career. What a contrast between one who has selected rightly and one who has not; one is a blessing to himself, his family, and the world; the other, either a machine-like workman, having no interest in what he is doing, or is a load to his friends and a burden on the community. Many people with talents, the exercise of which would place them in the front rank of some of the higher callings, are living in obscurity, filling some menial place, which they dropped into by chance or accident, ignorant of the talents with which God has endowed them. Let every man, woman, and youth read this book and profit by it, and undertake only that which they can do best.

The author was fully qualified for his task, having been engaged wholly and actively as editor and lecturer, and in the practical application of mental science to every-day life for forty years, affording opportunities for making the fullest observations and original investigations on the human mind and its capacity.

The book is handsomely bound in extra muslin, with gilt and ink stamps. Price, by mail, postpaid, $1.50. Address

FOWLER & WELLS CO., Publishers, 775 Broadway, New York.

HOW TO LEARN PHRENOLOGY.

We are frequently asked: In what way can a practical knowledge of Phrenology be obtained? In answering this we must say, that the best results can be obtained by taking a thorough course of instruction at the American Institute of Phrenology; but where this is not practical, the published textbooks on the subject should be carefully studied. To meet the wants of those who wish to pursue the subject personally and become familiar with the application of the subject to the various sides of life, we have arranged the following list of books, called

THE STUDENT'S SET:

Brain and Mind; or, Mental Science Considered in Accordance with the Principles of Phrenology and in Relation to Modern Physiology. Illustrated. By H. S. DRAYTON, A. M., M. D., and JAS. McNIEL, A. M. $1.50.

Forty Years in Phrenology; Embracing Recollections of History, Anecdotes, and Experience.$1.50.

How to Read Character. A New Illustrated Handbook of Phrenology and Physiognomy, for students and examiners, with a Chart for recording the sizes of the different organs of the brain in the delineation of character; with upward of one hundred and seventy engravings. $1.25.

Popular Physiology. A Familiar Exposition of the Structures, Functions, and Relations of the Human System and the preservation of health. $1.00.

The Phrenological Bust, showing the location of each of the Organs. Large size. $1.00.

New Physiognomy; or, Signs of Character, as manifested through temperament and external forms, and especially in the "Human Face Divine." With more than one thousand illustrations. $5.00.

Choice of Pursuits; or, What to do and Why. Describing seventy-five trades and professions, and the temperaments and talents required for each. Also, how to educate on phrenological principles—each man for his proper work; together with portraits and biographies of many successful thinkers and workers. $1.75.

Constitution of Man; Considered in relation to external objects. The only authorized American edition. With twenty engravings and a portrait of the author. $1.25.

Heads and Faces and How to STUDY THEM. A manual of Phrenology and physiognomy for the people. By NELSON SIZER and H. S. DRAYTON. Oct., paper,40c.

This list is commended to those who wish to pursue the subject at home, and to those who propose to attend the Institute.

Either of the above will be sent on receipt of price, or the complete "STUDENT'S SET," amounting to $14.65, will be sent by express for $10.00. Address,

FOWLER & WELLS CO., Publishers, 775 Broadway, New York.

[PORTRAITS FROM LIFE, IN "HEADS AND FACES."]

HUMAN-NATURE.

If you want something to read that will interest you more thoroughly than any book you have ever read, send for a copy of HEADS AND FACES, a new Manual of Character Reading for the people. It will show you how to read people as you would a book, and see if they are inclined to be good, upright, honest, true, kind, charitable, loving, joyous, happy and trustworthy people, such as you would like to know; or are they by nature untrustworthy, treacherous and cruel, uncharitable and hard-hearted, fault-finding, jealous, domineering people whom you would not want to have intimate with yourselves or your families.

A knowledge of Human-Nature will enable you to judge of all this at sight, and to choose for yourselves and children such companions as will tend to make you and them better, purer, more noble and ambitious to do and to be right, and would save many disappointments in social and business relations. It will aid in choosing and governing servants, training children, and deciding whom to trust in all the affairs of life. If you would know people without waiting to become acquainted with them, read HEADS AND FACES and How to Study Them, a new manual of Character Reading, by Prof. Nelson Sizer, the Examiner in the phrenological office of Fowler & Wells Co., New York, and H. S. Drayton, M. D., Editor of the PHRENOLOGICAL JOURNAL. The authors know what they are writing about. Prof. Sizer having devoted more than forty years almost exclusively to the reading of character and he here lays down the rules employed by him in his professional work.

The study of this subject is most fascinating, and you will certainly be much interested in it. Send for this book, which is the most comprehensive and popular work ever published for the price, 25,000 copies having been sold the first year. Contains 200 large octavo pages, 250 Portraits and other Illustrations.

We will send it carefully by mail, postpaid, on receipt of price, only 40 cents in paper, or $1.00 in cloth binding. Address

Fowler & Wells Co., Publishers, 775 Broadway, New York.

A Choice of Premiums.

THE
PHRENOLOGICAL JOURNAL

Is widely known in America and Europe, having been before the reading world fifty years, and occupying a place in literature exclusively its own, viz., the study of HUMAN NATURE in all its phases, including Phrenology, Physiognomy, Ethnology, Physiology, etc., to- gether with the "SCIENCE OF HEALTH," and no expense will be spared to make it the best publication for general circulation, tending always to make men better physically, mentally, and morally. Parents and teachers should read the JOURNAL, that they may bet- ter know how to govern and train their children. Young people should read the JOURNAL, that they may make the most of themselves. It has long met with the hearty approval of the press and the people.

TERMS.—The JOURNAL is published monthly at $2.00 a year, or 20 cents a Number. To each new subscriber is given either the BUST or CHART Premium described above. When the Premiums are sent, 15 cents extra must be received with each sub- scription to pay postage on the JOURNAL and the expense of boxing and packing the Bust, which will be sent by express, or No. 2, a smaller size, or the Chart Premium, will be sent by mail, post-paid.

Send amount in P. O. Orders, P. N., Drafts on New York, or in Registered Letters. Postage-stamps will be received. AGENTS WANTED. Send 10 cents for Specimen Num- ber. Premium List, Posters, etc. Address

FOWLER & WELLS CO., Publishers, 775 Broadway, New York.

A PLACE OF INTEREST.

The Phrenological Cabinet, located at 775 Broadway, New York, above 9th street, and directly opposite "Stewart's," contains a large and interesting collection including hundreds of Busts, Casts, Portraits, and Sketches of Men and Women, noted and notorious, from all classes, including Statesmen, Soldiers, Lawyers, Divines, Inventors, Philanthropists, etc., with Murderers, Pirates, and others from the lower walks of life, with many recent additions, and is kept open and free to visitors during all business hours. This we do for the purpose of affording facilities for the study of HUMAN-NATURE and in order to interest the people in this subject, making it really a very important educational center. Here the visitor can study heads and faces at leisure, compare the size and shape of the busts of the world's celebrities, which are carefully arranged and catalogued, with a competent person always in attendance to answer inquiries, and to afford facilities for their proper examination and study. The public, and especially those interested in the subject, are cordially invited to visit our rooms without feeling under the slightest obligation to make purchases, for if the people become interested, we have accomplished our purpose in affording them these facilities. Come and examine the world's men of genius, of talent, and of crime, and become familiar with Heads and Faces and what they mean.

This Cabinet belongs to the AMERICAN INSTITUTE OF PHRENOLOGY, an institution chartered by the legislature of the State of New York for the purpose of giving instruction and public lectures on this subject. For full particulars as to the class held each year and for Institute Extra, address

FOWLER & WELLS CO.,
775 Broadway, New York.

A STORY WORTH READING.

About Human Nature.

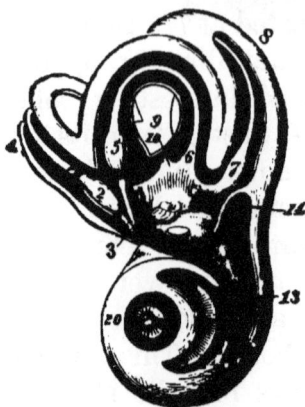

We have recently published a volume containing a story of Human Nature which will be found of interest. It is called "The MAN WONDERFUL in the HOUSE BEAUTIFUL," and is an allegory, teaching the principles of Physiology and Hygiene, and the effects of Stimulants and Narcotics. The House is the Body, in which the Foundations are the Bones, the Walls are Muscles, the Skin and Hair the Siding and Shingles, the head an Observatory in which are found a pair of Telescopes, and radiating from it are the nerves which are compared to a Telegraph, while communications are kept up with the Kitchen, Dining-room, Pantry, Laundry, etc. The House is heated with a Furnace. There are also Mysterious Chambers, and the whole is protected by a Burglar Alarm. In studying the inhabitant of the House, the "Man Wonderful," we learn of his growth, development, and habits of the guests whom he introduces. He finds that some of them are friends, others are doubtful acquaintances, and some decidedly wicked. Under this form, we ascertain the effects of Food and Drink, Narcotics and Stimulants.

It is a wonderful book, and placed in the hands of children will lead them to the study of Physiology and Hygiene, and the Laws of Life and Health in a way that will never be forgotten. The book will prove of great interest even to adults and those familiar with the subject. The authors, Drs. C. B. and Mary A. Allen, are both regular physicians, and therefore the work is accurate and on a scientific basis. "Science in Story" has never been presented in a more attractive form. It is universally admitted that a large proportion of sickness comes from violations of the laws of Life and Health, and therefore it is important that this subject should be understood by all, as in this way we may become familiar with all the avoidable causes of disease. The reading of this book will very largely accomplish this end. It will be sent securely by mail, prepaid, on receipt of price, which is only $1.50.   Address

Fowler & Wells Co., Publishers, 775 Broadway, New York.

THE LABYRINTH.

PHYSICAL CULTURE.

For Home and School. Scientific and Practical. By D. L. Dowd, Professor of Physical Culture. 322 12mo. pages. 300 Illustrations. Fine Binding. Price $1.50.

CONTENTS.

Physical Culture, Scientific and Practical, for the Home and School. Pure Air and Foul Air.

Questions Constantly Being Asked:

No 1. Does massage treatment strengthen muscular tissue?
No. 2. Are boat-racing and horseback-riding good exercises?
No. 3. Are athletic sports conducive to health?
No. 4. Why do you object to developing with heavy weights?
No. 5. How long a time will it take to reach the limit of development?
No. 6. Is there a limit to muscular development, and is it possible to gain an abnormal development?
No. 7. What is meant by being muscle bound?
No. 8. Why are some small men stronger than others of nearly double their size?
No. 9. Why is a person taller with less weight in the morning than in the evening?
No. 10. How should a person breathe while racing or walking up-stairs or up-hill?
No. 11. Is there any advantage gained by weighting the shoes of sprinters and horses?
No. 12. What kind of food is best for us to eat?
No. 13. What form of bathing is best?
No. 14. How can I best reduce my weight, or how increase it?
No. 15. Can you determine the size of one's lungs by blowing in a spirometer?

Personal Experience of the Author in Physical Training. Physical Culture for the Voice. Practice of Deep Breathing. Facial and Neck Development. A few Hints for the Complexion. The Graceful and Ungraceful Figure, and Improvement of Deformities, such as Bow-Leg, Knock-Knee, Wry-Neck, Round Shoulders, Lateral Curvature of the Spine, etc. A few Brief Rules. The Normal Man. Specific Exercises for the Development of Every Set of Muscles of the Body, Arms and Legs, also Exercises for Deepening and Broadening the Chest and Strengthening the Lungs.

These 34 Specific Exercises are each illustrated by a full length figure (taken from life) showing the set of muscles in contraction, which can be developed by each of them.] Dumb Bell Exercises. Ten Appendices showing the relative gain of pupils from 9 years of age to 40.

All who value Health, Strength and Happiness should procure and read this work; it will be found by far the best work ever written on this important subject. Sent by mail, postpaid, on receipt of price. $1.50.

Address, **Fowler & Wells Co., Publishers, 775 Broadway, New York.**

www.ingramcontent.com/pod-product-compliance
Lightning Source LLC
Chambersburg PA
CBHW030909270326
41929CB00008B/631